DETOXIFICATION
Toxic Work Atmosphere

*Breaking Free from Toxicity and
Reclaiming Your Well-being
in the Workplace*

Mercedes E.O. Monden

Toxic Work Atmosphere

© 2024 by Mercedes E.O. Monden.

All rights reserved.

This book, Detoxification: Toxic Work Atmosphere, and all its contents are protected by copyright law. No part of this publication may be reproduced, distributed, or transmitted in any form or by any means, including photocopying, recording, or other electronic or mechanical methods, without the prior written permission of the author, except in the case of brief quotations embodied in critical reviews and certain other noncommercial uses permitted by copyright law.

For permission requests, please contact the author at: publishing@mercedesmonden.world

Unauthorized reproduction, use, or distribution of this book, or any portion of it, may result in legal action, including but not limited to, claims for damages, injunctive relief, and statutory penalties as allowed under applicable copyright law.

Dedication

This book is dedicated to everyone who has ever felt trapped, undervalued, or overlooked in a toxic work environment. To those who have endured the emotional and mental toll of toxicity but continue to rise above it—this is for you. May this book be a beacon of hope, strength, and empowerment on your journey to reclaiming your well-being and purpose.

To my family, friends, and ministry, thank you for your unwavering support, love, and belief in my mission to help others. You inspire me every day to continue my work. A special thanks to my youngest daughter, Jaylinn Grace Monden—thank you for challenging and encouraging me to keep writing!

And above all, to God, whose wisdom, guidance, and grace have been my foundation and source of strength throughout this journey. May this book serve as a vessel for His healing and transformation in the lives of all who read it.

Preface

In my journey as a leader, pastor, and advocate for personal and spiritual growth, I've had the privilege of working with individuals from all walks of life—many of whom have shared stories of their struggles in toxic work environments. The stories are often similar: feelings of isolation, exhaustion, frustration, and uncertainty. People find themselves in situations where their value is diminished, their contributions are ignored, and their sense of purpose eroded. These stories, along with my own experiences, are what inspired me to write this book, Detoxification: Toxic Work Atmosphere.

Workplace toxicity is a silent epidemic, and its effects reach far beyond the confines of the office. The emotional and psychological tolls that a toxic work environment can take are profound, affecting not only one's professional life but also their personal well-being, relationships, and even their faith. Over time, I have seen how detrimental such environments can be, leading to burnout, lost potential, and worst of all, a loss of self-worth.

In my role as the founder of Breath of Holies Worldwide Outreach Ministries and leader of several empowerment movements, I have always believed in the power of transformation. Whether it is through faith, personal growth, or professional development, we all possess the ability to change our circumstances and reclaim the peace and joy we deserve. This belief is at the heart of this book.

Detoxification: Toxic Work Atmosphere is meant to be more than just a guide for surviving toxic environments—it is a resource for healing, empowerment, and growth. In these pages, you will find strategies for identifying and addressing toxicity, practical steps for safeguarding your mental health, and tools for rebuilding your professional life after leaving a negative environment. Whether you are dealing with difficult managers, toxic colleagues, or systemic discrimination, this book offers a roadmap to navigate those challenges with strength and clarity.

It's my hope that this book will empower you to break free from toxicity and step into a healthier, more fulfilling professional life. You are not alone in your struggles, and there are solutions. Through self-awareness, reflection, and a commitment to creating change, you can detoxify your work atmosphere and find joy, purpose, and peace in your career.

As you read through the following chapters, I encourage you to take heart. Change is possible, and with the right mindset and tools, you can create a positive work environment that nurtures your spirit, aligns with your values, and supports your personal and professional growth. Thank you for allowing me to be part of your journey. It's time to reclaim the work life you deserve.

— Mercedes E.O. Monden

Acknowledgements

First and foremost, I would like to express my deepest gratitude to God, whose grace, wisdom, and unwavering love have guided me throughout this journey. This book would not exist without His strength and constant presence in my life. I pray that His healing touch reaches every reader through these pages.

To my family, thank you for your endless love, patience, and support. Your belief in me has been the anchor that has kept me grounded through every challenge and triumph. Jaylinn Grace Monden, my youngest daughter, you inspire me in ways you may never fully realize. Your encouragement, curiosity, and insistence that I continue writing has been one of the greatest motivations in completing this book.

To my friends and ministry family, your support has been invaluable. Thank you for believing in my vision, lifting me up when the journey felt overwhelming, and for being a constant source of strength and joy. Breath of Holies Worldwide Outreach Ministries and Royal Crown Church, your faith and trust in my mission have inspired me to keep moving forward with purpose and passion.

A heartfelt thanks to the leaders, mentors, and colleagues who have shaped my professional journey and provided insights that have influenced this book. Your wisdom and guidance helped me better understand the dynamics of the workplace, and I am truly grateful.

Finally, to every reader who picks up this book, thank you for allowing me to be a part of your journey. I wrote this book with the hope that it will provide you with the tools, strength, and encouragement needed to navigate and heal from toxic environments. You are the reason for this work, and it is my honor to walk alongside you in the pursuit of empowerment, healing, and transformation.

Table of Contents

Introduction 1
  The Urgency of Workplace Detoxification
Chapter 1 4
  Understanding Toxic Work Environments
Chapter 2 7
  The Toxic Manager The Role of Leadership in Workplace Culture
Chapter 3 16
  Recognizing Toxic Colleagues
Chapter 4 21
  Are You Contributing to Workplace Toxicity?
Chapter 5 36
  Mental Health in a Toxic Environment
Chapter 6 42
  Breaking Free How to Escape or Manage a Toxic Environment
Chapter 7 52
  Legal Rights and Workplace Protections (EU and COA Law)
Chapter 8 59

Recognizing and Confronting Discrimination

Chapter 9 66

Combating Racism in the Workplace

Chapter 10 73

Pros and Cons of Exposing Toxicity

Chapter 11 80

Rebuilding After the Toxicity

Chapter 12 87

Preventing Toxicity in the Future

Conclusion 94

The Path to a Healthier Work Life

Bonus Read 98

Daily Affirmations for Workplace Healing

Appendix 100

End Notes 103

About the Author 107

INTRODUCTION

The Urgency of Workplace Detoxification

Importance of Mental Well-being in the Workplace

In today's fast-paced and competitive work environments, employees are often required to balance high levels of productivity, long hours, and personal well-being. Mental health, however, is often sidelined in the quest for success and efficiency. Yet, mental well-being is the foundation of not only personal fulfillment but also professional performance. Employees who are mentally healthy are more productive, creative, and engaged.

This section will explore how the stress and strain of working in a toxic environment can erode an individual's mental health. Chronic exposure to negativity, unhealthy work dynamics, and poor leadership can result in anxiety, depression, burnout, and even physical health problems. It is imperative to recognize that protecting mental health is just as important as safeguarding physical health in the workplace. When an individual's mental health suffers, it affects every aspect of their life, including their ability to contribute meaningfully at work.

Mercedes E.O. Monden

Why Workplace Toxicity Must Be Addressed Now

Toxic work environments are not just harmful to individual employees—they are detrimental to entire organizations. Research consistently shows that toxicity in the workplace leads to lower productivity, higher absenteeism, and increased employee turnover. Toxicity damages the trust and collaboration necessary for team success and innovation, which are critical in today's ever-evolving global economy.

As more people become aware of their rights and the importance of mental well-being, there is a growing demand for workplaces that foster positive, healthy environments. Moreover, legal frameworks are evolving to hold organizations accountable for toxic behaviors such as bullying, harassment, and discrimination. Now, more than ever, addressing toxicity is not just a moral obligation but a strategic necessity for companies aiming to attract and retain talent. This book will serve as a guide to help both employees and organizations take proactive steps to identify and eliminate toxicity before it causes lasting damage.

Purpose and Structure of This Book.

This book is designed as a practical resource for anyone struggling with or wanting to better understand toxic work environments. Whether you are dealing with a toxic manager, difficult colleagues, or systemic issues such as discrimination and racism, this guide will equip you with the tools and knowledge to recognize, confront, and break free from workplace toxicity. It will also help you assess your own behaviors to ensure you are not contributing to toxicity unintentionally.

The book is structured into 13 chapters, each addressing different facets of toxicity in the workplace. It starts by defining what a toxic work environment looks like and how to recognize toxic managers and colleagues. From there, it moves into actionable strategies for protecting your mental health, legal guidance on your rights under EU and COA law, and specific advice for dealing with discrimination and racism in the workplace. Finally, it provides insights into rebuilding your career and emotional well-being after escaping a toxic environment, as well as guidance on preventing workplace toxicity from arising in the first place.

By the end of this book, you will have a clear understanding of the tools available to help you navigate toxicity in the workplace. You will be empowered to make informed decisions that prioritize your mental health and professional integrity, while also recognizing how to contribute to a healthier work environment. This book is your detoxification guide, giving you the power to reclaim your work life and protect your future.

CHAPTER 1

Understanding Toxic Work Environments

What Defines a Toxic Work Environment?

A toxic work environment is more than just a stressful workplace or a demanding boss—it is a pervasive culture of negativity that affects everyone within it. Toxicity in the workplace can manifest in many ways, from open hostility and bullying to subtler forms of manipulation and exclusion. What makes a work environment truly toxic is the consistent presence of harmful behaviors, attitudes, and practices that undermine the well-being of employees and the health of the organization.

In a toxic workplace, employees may experience persistent stress, fear, or anxiety. There is often a lack of support from leadership, poor communication, and an absence of trust between colleagues. Toxic environments breed insecurity, low morale, and frustration, with employees feeling undervalued, disrespected, or overworked. This chapter will define the key traits of a toxic work environment and differentiate them from workplaces that may be challenging but not necessarily harmful. Understanding these distinctions is crucial in diagnosing workplace toxicity and determining the appropriate course of action.

Identifying the Signs: Subtle and Obvious

Toxic work environments do not always reveal themselves immediately. Some forms of toxicity are glaringly obvious, such as open conflict, harassment, or public shaming. In these cases, the damage to employee morale and productivity is clear, and the toxic dynamics are often well-known, even if left unaddressed by management.

However, toxicity can also take more subtle forms. These are often harder to detect but equally damaging. Signs might include:

1. Passive-aggressive behavior from colleagues or supervisors
2. Unclear expectations or constantly shifting goals, leading to confusion and frustration
3. A culture where employees are pitted against each other or encouraged to compete in unhealthy ways
4. Excessive micromanagement, which strips employees of autonomy and trust
5. Non-inclusive practices where certain employees are consistently left out of decision-making or opportunities for growth

These subtle signs create an undercurrent of negativity and can lead to high levels of stress, disengagement, and burnout over time. In this section, you will learn how to recognize both the overt and covert indicators of workplace toxicity so that you can take action before the damage becomes irreparable.

The Impact of Workplace Toxicity on Employees and Organizations

Toxic work environments have far-reaching effects, impacting not only the emotional and mental health of employees but also the overall success of the organization. For employees, constant exposure to toxic behaviors can lead to:

- Burnout, characterized by emotional exhaustion, cynicism, and decreased job performance.
- Anxiety and depression, often stemming from a sense of helplessness, lack of control, or fear of job insecurity.
- Physical health problems, such as stress-related illnesses, headaches, and sleep disorders.
- A loss of confidence and self-worth, particularly if the toxicity comes in the form of bullying, gaslighting, or unfair criticism.

On the organizational level, toxicity erodes the fabric of the company, leading to a host of challenges:

- **Increased turnover:** Employees in toxic environments are far more likely to leave, resulting in costly turnover rates and a loss of institutional knowledge.
- **Decreased productivity:** Toxic work cultures make it difficult for employees to stay motivated or focused, directly impacting output and profitability.
- **Damaged reputation:** Companies known for toxicity struggle to attract top talent, damaging their ability to compete in their industries.
- **Stagnation in innovation and creativity:** A culture of fear stifles open communication, problem-solving, and collaboration, limiting the organization's potential for growth.

This chapter will delve into specific examples of how workplace toxicity plays out and how its consequences can cascade through the workforce and organization. It will also highlight why early intervention and prevention are vital to preserving both employee well-being and the overall health of the company. By understanding these impacts, employees and leaders alike can begin to take meaningful steps toward detoxifying their work environments and fostering a more positive culture.

CHAPTER 2

The Toxic Manager
The Role of Leadership in Workplace Culture

---•• — ● — ••---

Characteristics of a Toxic Manager.

A manager's behavior and leadership style can either create a thriving, positive work culture or lead to a toxic environment that demoralizes employees. Toxic managers exhibit specific traits that undermine trust, communication, and productivity. Some of the most common characteristics of a toxic manager include:

   a. **Micromanagement:** Constantly hovering over employees, scrutinizing every minor detail, and not trusting staff to complete tasks without close supervision. This erodes employees' autonomy and confidence.
   b. **Manipulative behavior:** Playing employees against each other, withholding important information, or making promises with no intention of fulfilling them to gain control over team members.

c. **Lack of empathy:** A toxic manager typically has little regard for employees' emotional well-being, showing insensitivity to their personal or professional challenges.
d. **Blame-shifting:** Instead of taking responsibility for their own mistakes or decisions, toxic managers blame their team for any failures, even when the fault lies with their leadership.
e. **Favoritism:** Treating certain employees better than others, providing more opportunities or leniency to a select few, which can create resentment and division within the team.
f. **Unrealistic expectations:** Overloading employees with excessive work without considering their capacity or personal time, setting them up for burnout and frustration.

These behaviors not only create immediate stress for employees but also disrupt team cohesion and long-term organizational success. In this section, you will learn to identify these traits in your own workplace and understand the impact they can have on the work environment.

How Toxic Leadership Fosters a Negative Work Culture.

Toxic leadership has a trickle-down effect that contaminates the entire workplace. Managers are not just responsible for delegating tasks—they set the tone for communication, collaboration, and the overall work atmosphere. A toxic manager's actions can lead to:

a. **Breakdown in communication:** Employees may become fearful of sharing ideas or concerns, either because they are constantly criticized or because they feel unheard. This creates a communication barrier that stifles innovation and collaboration.

b. **Fear-based culture:** When managers use intimidation, threats, or passive-aggressive tactics to control their team, employees work in a state of fear. This fear prevents them from taking risks, speaking up, or addressing problems, which can lead to stagnation and low morale.
c. **Low employee engagement:** Toxic leadership makes employees feel undervalued and unappreciated. Over time, they lose motivation to go above and beyond, resulting in decreased productivity and engagement.
d. **High turnover:** Employees who feel oppressed or demoralized under toxic leadership are more likely to seek employment elsewhere, resulting in higher turnover and recruitment costs for the organization.

In contrast, supportive and effective leadership fosters open communication, trust, and mutual respect, leading to higher engagement, retention, and overall performance. Toxic managers not only poison individual relationships but also damage the organizational culture in ways that can be difficult to reverse.

Case Studies of Toxic vs. Supportive Management.

This section will explore real-world case studies that illustrate the stark differences between toxic and supportive management styles. These examples will provide insights into how managers' behaviors impact the broader work culture:

- Case Study 1: The Micromanager

A manager at a tech company insisted on controlling every detail of their team's projects, refusing to delegate even minor tasks. The result was burnout across the team, with employees feeling suffocated and disengaged. High turnover followed, with the organization ultimately losing valuable talent and productivity.

- Case Study 2: The Supportive Manager

At a healthcare startup, a manager prioritized employee well-being by offering flexible hours and encouraging open communication. This manager took the time to understand individual team members' strengths and trusted them to complete their work independently. The team thrived, consistently exceeding their goals, and turnover was low.

- Case Study 3: The Blame Shifter

In a retail company, the toxic manager often blamed their team when things went wrong, taking credit only when successes were achieved. This led to a fear-driven culture where employees were reluctant to experiment or offer ideas, stifling growth and creativity. Eventually, several key team members resigned due to frustration with the lack of accountability and support.

Through these case studies, readers will see the real-life impact of toxic leadership and the positive change that supportive management can bring to workplace culture.

How to Deal with a Toxic Manager:

Dealing with a toxic manager can feel overwhelming, especially when their behavior directly affects your daily well-being. However, there are strategies you can employ to protect yourself and navigate this challenging situation:

1. Document everything: Keep a detailed record of any toxic behaviors, such as unreasonable demands, inappropriate comments, or instances of favoritism or manipulation. This documentation will be crucial if you need to escalate the issue to higher management or HR. (Only facts)

2. Set boundaries: While it can be difficult to stand up to a toxic manager, setting clear boundaries regarding your workload, personal time, or communication expectations can help protect your mental health. Be professional but firm when communicating these boundaries.

3. Seek support: Build a support network of trusted colleagues, mentors, or even HR representatives who can offer advice and support when dealing with your manager. In some cases, talking to HR may be the appropriate next step, especially if the manager's behavior violates company policies.

4. Use conflict management techniques: Try using non-confrontational approaches to resolve issues with your toxic manager. This could involve practicing active listening, using "I" statements instead of accusatory language, and staying calm during conflicts. These strategies can help reduce tension and maintain professionalism.

5. Know your rights: Understand your legal protections under EU and COA laws regarding workplace bullying, harassment, and unfair treatment. If your manager's actions violate your legal rights, you may need to involve legal counsel to ensure you are protected.

6. Decide when to leave: Sometimes, the best solution to a toxic manager is to leave the environment altogether. If you've tried addressing the situation internally and seen no improvement, it may be time to prioritize your well-being by seeking employment elsewhere.

The Danger of a Manager Who Cannot Make Informed and Firm Decisions.

We often discuss toxic managers in terms of their tendency to micromanage employees, but we sometimes overlook another critical issue—managers who are unable to make well-informed, decisive decisions. This form of leadership, characterized by indecisiveness and a lack of conviction, can be just as harmful to the workplace as micromanagement.

A manager who is unable to make informed and firm decisions poses several risks to both the team and the overall organization. When a leader is unsure or hesitant in their decision-making, it creates confusion, slows progress, and leaves employees feeling uncertain about their roles and responsibilities.

Projects stagnate, goals become unclear, and morale declines as employees lose confidence in their leader's ability to guide the team effectively.

In addition, an indecisive manager often becomes dependent on others for direction, which can lead to poor judgment calls influenced by the wrong people or incomplete information. Without a clear and strong decision-making process, the team is left rudderless, and any attempt to innovate or progress can be stifled by the constant need for direction that never materializes. Ultimately, the workplace culture suffers as employees feel unsupported, directionless, and powerless to make meaningful contributions.

How Should You Work with a Manager Who Doesn't Have a Mind of Their Own?

Working with a manager who lacks independent thinking is a delicate balance. When a manager is overly dependent on others or seems to lack the confidence to lead, employees often find themselves taking on the role of guiding the manager rather than receiving direction from them. This can create frustration, especially when critical decisions are delayed or deferred to others.

To navigate this situation:

1. Be Proactive: Take the initiative by presenting clear, well-researched solutions to problems. The more prepared and confident you are, the more likely the manager will follow your lead.

2. Offer Constructive Support: Recognize that this manager might struggle with confidence. Try offering subtle guidance without undermining their authority. Frame your suggestions in a way that empowers them to make decisions, for example, by presenting options and explaining the potential outcomes.

3. Document Communication: Keep clear records of your interactions and decisions. This ensures accountability and can protect you if the manager's indecisiveness leads to confusion or issues later on.

4. Set Boundaries: If the manager's indecisiveness starts to affect your work or mental health, it's important to set boundaries. Ensure you're not overextending yourself by trying to compensate for their lack of leadership.

Dealing with a Well-Meaning Manager Whose Trusted Advisor is the Predator.

One of the most challenging dynamics in the workplace is dealing with a manager who, despite having good intentions, is surrounded by toxic influences—particularly when their trusted advisor is the source of the problem. This advisor may be the real "predator," subtly manipulating the manager and shaping decisions in ways that harm the team.

In such cases, employees often find themselves caught between a well-meaning manager and a toxic influencer. They may hesitate to speak up because they know that their concerns will either not be taken seriously or will be filtered through the lens of the toxic advisor.

To handle this situation:

1. Carefully Assess the Manager's Influence: Pay attention to how much autonomy the manager really has versus how much sway the advisor holds. If it becomes clear that the advisor is controlling key decisions, it may be necessary to approach the manager indirectly, or work through other channels to avoid confrontation.

2. Build Trust with the Manager: Strengthen your direct relationship with the manager. Establishing open lines of communication can help you bypass the influence of the toxic advisor. If the manager trusts you more, they may be more open to your input and less reliant on the predatory advisor.

3. Document Concerns and Incidents: If the advisor's toxic behavior is harming the workplace, keep a detailed record of specific incidents. This can be critical if you need to escalate the issue to HR or higher management.

Is This a Lost Cause?

This situation can feel like a lost cause, especially when you know more about what's happening than your manager does. The toxic advisor might be skilled at gaslighting or manipulating situations to ensure that the manager doesn't see the full picture. However, this doesn't mean it's impossible to overcome. While it may seem like the manager is unaware, building trust with them and subtly offering alternative perspectives can help chip away at the influence of the toxic advisor.

It is crucial to maintain persistence and professionalism, and to avoid direct confrontations with the advisor unless necessary. If all else fails, escalating the issue or considering alternative career paths may be required to protect your well-being.

How to Overcome Gaslighting by Your Manager

Gaslighting, a manipulative tactic where someone causes you to question your reality, is an insidious form of psychological abuse that some managers use to maintain control. When a manager gaslights you, they may downplay your achievements, deny previous conversations, or shift blame to make you doubt your own experiences.

To overcome gaslighting:

1. Document Everything: One of the most effective ways to combat gaslighting is to keep thorough documentation. Record meetings, save emails, and note any decisions that are made. This provides a factual record that can help you push back against any attempts to rewrite history or manipulate facts.

2. Trust Your Instincts: Gaslighting works by making you doubt yourself. It's important to stay grounded and trust your instincts. If something feels wrong, it likely is. Don't let your manager undermine your sense of reality.

Detoxification: Toxic Work Atmosphere

3. Seek External Validation: Talk to trusted colleagues or mentors outside the situation. They can provide perspective and help you validate your experiences, which is essential in countering the effects of gaslighting.

4. Confront the Behavior Calmly: If you're comfortable doing so, calmly confront the manager. Use facts and documentation to back up your statements, and avoid getting emotional. State the specific behaviors you've observed and how they differ from reality.

5. Set Boundaries: If gaslighting persists, it's important to establish clear professional boundaries. Limit your exposure to the manager's manipulation as much as possible. If necessary, escalate the issue to HR or another higher authority.

By staying vigilant, documenting interactions, and trusting yourself, you can resist the corrosive effects of gaslighting and maintain your professionalism in the face of this manipulative behavior.

This piece is designed to empower you, that is why I amplified the key issues surrounding indecisive managers, toxic advisors, and gaslighting while offering practical solutions for navigating these difficult situations. It provides a deeper analysis and offers tools for handling complex workplace dynamics effectively.

CHAPTER 3

Recognizing Toxic Colleagues

— •• — • — •• —

What Makes a Colleague Toxic?

Toxic colleagues can be just as damaging to workplace well-being as toxic managers, often because their behavior can be insidious and difficult to address directly. A toxic colleague isn't simply someone with a difficult personality—they actively disrupt work, erode trust, and contribute to a negative environment that affects everyone around them. Common traits of toxic colleagues include:

a. **Chronic negativity:** Constantly complaining about work, the organization, or other colleagues without offering solutions. Their pessimism can dampen morale and drain energy from the team.

b. **Backstabbing and gossiping:** Spreading rumors, talking negatively about others behind their backs, and creating divisions within the team. This behavior fosters mistrust and breeds a hostile work atmosphere.

c. **Manipulative or self-serving behavior:** These colleagues prioritize their own interests at the expense of others. They may take credit for work they didn't do, undermine others to elevate themselves, or use manipulation to get ahead.

d. **Passive-aggressiveness:** Toxic colleagues often avoid direct confrontation but express their hostility through subtle, undermining behavior. This could include leaving snide comments, purposefully withholding important information, or making backhanded compliments.
e. **Lack of accountability:** Toxic colleagues deflect responsibility for their actions, blaming others when things go wrong, and never acknowledging their own mistakes. This creates frustration and chaos within teams, as others are left to clean up the mess.

Recognizing these behaviors early on is essential to protecting yourself from their negative impact. Toxic colleagues can have a ripple effect on team cohesion, morale, and even productivity. In this section, you'll learn to identify the warning signs of toxic behavior in your coworkers and understand the broader implications for your work environment.

The Fine Line Between a Difficult and Toxic Coworker

Not every difficult colleague is toxic, and it's important to distinguish between the two. A difficult coworker may be hard to work with due to differences in communication styles, work habits, or personality clashes, but they are not inherently destructive. A difficult colleague might be overly critical, unorganized, or moody, but they do not necessarily undermine others or sabotage the work environment.

The key difference lies in intent and impact:

a. Difficult colleagues may present challenges but are still capable of collaboration and growth. They don't actively seek to harm others or undermine team dynamics.
b. Toxic colleagues, on the other hand, intentionally or recklessly damage relationships, manipulate situations to their benefit, and create a work environment that is harmful to others.

Understanding this distinction can help you determine the best approach for addressing problematic behavior. Dealing with a difficult coworker often requires improved communication and conflict resolution, whereas a toxic colleague may need stronger boundaries and more formal interventions.

In this section, we will discuss how to recognize the nuanced differences between a coworker who is merely challenging and one who is genuinely toxic. Identifying the right category will help you decide how to manage the situation effectively.

Strategies for Managing Interactions with Toxic Colleagues.

Once you've identified a toxic colleague, the next step is developing strategies to protect yourself and manage your interactions with them in a way that minimizes stress and conflict. The following are key strategies for dealing with toxic colleagues:

1. Set boundaries: Toxic colleagues often overstep personal and professional boundaries. Be clear and firm about what behavior you will and won't tolerate. For instance, if a toxic coworker frequently dumps tasks on you, you can politely but firmly say, "I'm at capacity with my current workload and won't be able to take that on."

2. Avoid engagement in negativity: Toxic colleagues thrive on drama, gossip, and negativity. When they attempt to pull you into these behaviors, don't engage. Politely excuse yourself from conversations that veer into harmful gossip or destructive complaining. Keep your focus on your work and positive aspects of the environment.

3. Limit interactions when possible: If you have the option, try to minimize unnecessary interactions with the toxic colleague. This might mean limiting non-work-related discussions or requesting to work on separate projects when feasible.

4. Use assertive communication: When addressing toxic behavior, use assertive, clear communication. Avoid passive or aggressive tones, and instead, be direct about your expectations and how their actions affect you. For example, "When you exclude me from important meetings, it impacts my ability to do my job effectively."

5. Document problematic behavior: Keep a written record of any inappropriate or harmful actions. If the toxic colleague's behavior escalates or becomes abusive, this documentation will be critical when reporting to HR or management. Include specific details about incidents, dates, and any witnesses.

6. Focus on your own professionalism: Toxic colleagues can bring out the worst in us if we let them. Make a conscious effort to maintain professionalism, even when the toxic coworker is attempting to provoke you. Stay focused on your work, and try not to let their behavior impact your performance or attitude.

7. Seek support from leadership or HR: If a toxic colleague's behavior is consistently disruptive and unmanageable, it may be necessary to escalate the issue to a manager or HR. Use the documentation you've gathered to present your case. Ensure that your complaint is framed around how the behavior impacts the team and the work environment rather than just a personal grievance.

8. Develop resilience: Dealing with toxic colleagues can be emotionally draining, but building resilience can help you manage stress more effectively. Focus on self-care, emotional well-being, and finding balance outside of work to prevent burnout from the negativity.

In this section, you will learn how to implement these strategies in your specific work context, from managing day-to-day interactions with toxic colleagues to deciding when and how to escalate issues to leadership or HR. The goal is to give you the tools to protect your own mental health and professional integrity while navigating a challenging work environment.

Mercedes E.O. Monden

This chapter will also empower you with a deeper understanding of what makes a colleague toxic, how to differentiate between a difficult coworker and a genuinely harmful one, and provide practical strategies to manage or mitigate the negative impact of toxic colleagues in your workplace.

CHAPTER 4

Are You Contributing to Workplace Toxicity?

Self-Reflection:

How You Might Be Toxic Without Realizing It.

It's easy to recognize toxic behaviors in others, but it's much harder to acknowledge that we may be contributing to workplace toxicity ourselves. Often, people exhibit toxic behaviors without realizing it, due to stress, lack of awareness, or ingrained habits from past environments. Self-reflection is a crucial first step toward understanding how your actions, attitudes, or communication styles might negatively affect those around you.

Consider how your behaviors align with common signs of toxicity:

a. Do you frequently complain or spread negativity at work without offering constructive solutions?
b. Do you tend to dominate conversations or dismiss others' ideas in meetings?

c. Are you prone to passive-aggressive comments, avoiding direct communication when conflicts arise?
   d. Do you take credit for group successes while deflecting blame when things go wrong?
   e. Are you overly critical of your colleagues' work, even when it's unnecessary or unhelpful?

These behaviors may not be intended to harm others, but their impact can still contribute to a toxic work environment. Toxicity often thrives in subtle actions—snide remarks, exclusion, or constant criticism. This section encourages readers to engage in honest self-assessment, reflecting on whether their actions might be damaging relationships, communication, or collaboration in the workplace.

Questions for self-reflection will be provided to help readers evaluate their own behavior:

1. Do I often feel frustrated or resentful toward colleagues?
2. Do I contribute more problems than solutions?
3. Do I listen to others with empathy, or do I dismiss their concerns?
4. Am I aware of how my tone, words, or actions affect others?

By looking inward, you can start to recognize toxic patterns in your own behavior and begin the process of change.

Personal Accountability and the Path to Change:

Once you've identified behaviors that may be contributing to toxicity, the next step is to take personal accountability. Recognizing your own role in creating a healthier work environment is empowering, as it puts you in control of positive change. Accountability begins with owning your actions, making no excuses, and understanding that everyone, regardless of their role or position, can influence the culture of their workplace.

Taking responsibility might involve:

a. Apologizing to colleagues you've wronged, whether intentionally or unintentionally. Acknowledging past mistakes shows maturity and helps rebuild trust.
b. Seeking feedback from coworkers or managers about how you can improve your communication or behavior. Be open to constructive criticism, as this is vital for growth.
c. Changing your approach to conflicts or challenging situations by responding more mindfully. This could mean addressing issues directly and respectfully instead of letting them fester into toxic behaviors like gossip or resentment.

You'll learn how to shift from defensiveness to openness, accepting that everyone makes mistakes but can also work toward improving their interactions with others. Accountability is not about being perfect, but about recognizing areas for improvement and committing to personal growth.

This section will provide practical exercises, such as:

a. Practicing active listening to ensure that you're truly hearing and considering others' perspectives.
b. Engaging in honest self-dialogue about the ways your behavior may be contributing to negative work dynamics and how you can adjust it.

The path to change isn't always easy, but with commitment, it is possible to shift away from toxic patterns and build more positive and productive workplace relationships.

Building Better Workplace Habits.

The key to transforming from a potential source of toxicity to a force for positivity lies in developing healthier workplace habits. Toxic behaviors can be replaced with constructive ones that foster collaboration, respect, and open communication. In this section, you will learn practical strategies for building habits that contribute to a healthier, more positive work culture.

1. Improve Communication: Make an effort to communicate openly, honestly, and constructively with your colleagues. Instead of criticizing or complaining, focus on giving feedback that's solution-oriented. Listen actively during discussions and make sure your communication style fosters respect and inclusion.

2. Practice Empathy: Empathy is one of the most powerful tools in creating a positive work environment. Taking the time to understand your colleagues' perspectives, challenges, and emotions can reduce conflict and promote cooperation. Simple acts of kindness and understanding can go a long way in building trust and strengthening relationships.

3. Manage Your Emotions: Stress, frustration, and pressure are common in the workplace, but how you handle these emotions can either contribute to or alleviate toxicity. Practice emotional regulation techniques, such as deep breathing or taking a pause before responding to difficult situations. Ensure that your emotional reactions don't harm those around you.

4. Be a Team Player: Workplace toxicity often stems from competition, cliques, or exclusion. Strive to be inclusive in your work. Encourage collaboration, support your colleagues' ideas, and help them succeed. A true team player lifts others up rather than pulling them down.

5. Foster a Growth Mindset: Instead of resisting change or being defensive about mistakes, embrace opportunities for learning and development. When challenges arise, see them as chances to grow, both personally and professionally. By adopting a mindset of continuous improvement, you can create a ripple effect that encourages others to do the same.

6. Respect Boundaries: Understanding and respecting the personal and professional boundaries of your colleagues is crucial. Ensure that you are not overstepping or expecting too much from others, and be mindful of work-life balance.

By consistently applying these habits, you will not only improve your own experience in the workplace but also contribute to a more positive and less toxic environment for everyone. This chapter will provide practical exercises and daily habits you can implement to foster a healthier work environment, such as journaling your progress, practicing gratitude, and learning conflict-resolution techniques.

Summary of this session.

The above session focuses on personal accountability and the importance of self-awareness in combating workplace toxicity. It emphasizes that while it's easy to point out toxic behaviors in others, the journey toward a healthier work culture begins with examining your own actions and making conscious changes. By embracing a growth mindset and implementing healthier workplace habits, readers can take charge of their behavior and make a positive impact on their professional environment. This not only improves their relationships with colleagues but also helps prevent future toxicity from taking root.

Intimidation and Bullying A Silent Threat in the Workplace.

There is a toxic trend in the workplace that is rarely discussed but affects countless individuals—intimidation. A few years ago, early in my career working with asylum seekers, I encountered this firsthand. It was my dream job, and anyone who knows me knows that I bring dedication, professionalism, and heart to everything I do. My work ethic is a balance of compassion and critical thinking, always ensuring I understand the full process of what I'm doing.

However, despite my commitment and passion for my work, I found myself the target of a systematic campaign of intimidation, alongside two other wonderful, elderly women who worked with me. We were harassed daily by a group of freelance male colleagues. What started as casual conversations quickly escalated into something far more intrusive and toxic. These colleagues constantly pressured us to discuss our faith, and over time, it became clear that their aim was to convert us to their own belief system. They weren't simply interested in a conversation; they were demanding that we justify our beliefs and consider their faith as superior.

The harassment didn't stop at religious discussions. These individuals fostered a hostile atmosphere for us and even targeted some of the residents we worked with, especially if the residents shared similar religious beliefs with the harassers but held slightly different interpretations. The message was clear: if you didn't believe exactly as they did, you became a target for intimidation and exclusion.

As the harassment intensified, so did my feelings of fear and anxiety. It wasn't just the daily intimidation that weighed on me, but also the knowledge that these colleagues had the favor and protection of our managers. It was well-known among the staff that these individuals had "wrapped the managers around their fingers." This power imbalance made the situation feel hopeless—why would the managers believe us over them? The constant anxiety and fear drained me emotionally, making it difficult to focus on the job I once loved.

Eventually, I gathered the courage to file an official complaint with the managers. I hoped that by bringing the issue to their attention, some action would be taken. However, rather than improving, the situation got worse. The managers may have addressed the issue while they were present, but the moment they were out of sight, the harassment escalated. We were shunned, isolated, and made to feel even more unwelcome. These colleagues went so far as to incite some of the residents against us, attempting to turn them into instruments of their intimidation. Fortunately, many of the residents refused to be part of this toxic behavior and even filed complaints themselves, expressing that they wanted no involvement in such an "atrocity."

From that experience, I learned an invaluable lesson: some topics, particularly those deeply personal, like religion, should be approached with extreme caution in the workplace, especially when there is potential for bullying or manipulation.

The Best Solutions for Workplace Bullying and Intimidation.

Workplace bullying, particularly when it involves intimidation or instigating hatred against a colleague, can have devastating effects—not just on the victim's mental and emotional well-being but also on the overall work culture. It creates an environment of fear, tension, and exclusion that is difficult to navigate. Here are key points to consider when addressing workplace bullying:

1. Workplace Bullying and Intimidation:

Bullying in the workplace is more than just personal conflict—it involves consistent, targeted behavior meant to demean, exclude, or intimidate an individual or group. It can take many forms, including:

a. **Verbal abuse:** Name-calling, derogatory comments, or belittling someone's work or beliefs.
b. **Social isolation:** Deliberately excluding someone from work-related activities or discussions.
c. **Undermining work:** Intentionally sabotaging someone's efforts or spreading false information to damage their reputation.
d. **Instigating hatred:** Turning other employees or, in this case, even residents, against someone through manipulation or spreading rumors.

2. The Consequences of Instigating Hatred:

When colleagues actively work to instigate hatred or resentment against others, it not only harms the victims but also poisons the entire work environment. Some of the key consequences include:

a. **Defamation of character:** False claims or rumors about a colleague's beliefs, work ethic, or personal life can damage their reputation, both professionally and personally.
b. **Emotional and psychological damage:** Victims of bullying often experience anxiety, depression, and a loss of self-esteem, which can lead to burnout and eventual withdrawal from the workforce.
c. **Decreased productivity:** A toxic environment drains morale and productivity, affecting not only the victim but also the broader team.
d. **Legal implications:** If bullying or harassment crosses into discrimination (based on religion, race, gender, etc.), there could be legal consequences for the employer, including lawsuits and penalties.

Legal Recourse for Workplace Bullying and Intimidation:

Workplace bullying and intimidation, particularly when it crosses into discrimination or harassment, may not only harm the individuals involved but can also have significant legal consequences for employers. In many countries, labor laws and anti-discrimination statutes provide legal protection for employees, holding companies accountable for failing to prevent or address such behavior.

When Bullying Becomes Discrimination:

If workplace bullying or intimidation is based on a protected characteristic such as religion, race, gender, age, disability, sexual orientation, or national origin, it can escalate from being a personal conflict to unlawful discrimination. Many countries, including those in the European Union and the United States, have laws that protect employees from discriminatory practices. These include:

a. **Title VII of the Civil Rights Act (United States):** Prohibits employment discrimination based on race, color, religion, sex, or national origin.
b. **The Equality Act (United Kingdom):** Provides legal protection from discrimination in the workplace based on various characteristics, including gender, disability, and age.
c. **The European Union Charter of Fundamental Rights:** Guarantees the right to non-discrimination and respect for dignity in employment across all EU member states.

Bullying becomes legally actionable when it targets an individual or group based on one of these protected characteristics, leading to hostile work environments, unfair treatment, or unequal employment opportunities.

Legal Consequences for Employers.

Employers have a legal obligation to maintain a safe, non-discriminatory work environment. Failing to address workplace bullying and intimidation can result in several legal consequences, including:

1. Lawsuits:

If an employer fails to act on reports of harassment or bullying, they may face lawsuits filed by the affected employees. In such cases, the employees can sue for:

a. **Compensation for emotional distress:** Victims can seek damages for the emotional and psychological harm caused by the bullying, including anxiety, depression, or trauma.

b. **Loss of wages or job opportunities:** If the bullying or harassment leads to job loss, demotion, or missed promotions, the employer may be required to compensate the victim for lost income or career progression.
c. **Punitive damages:** In cases where the employer's negligence or complicity in the bullying is severe, the court may award punitive damages to punish the employer and deter similar behavior in the future.

2. Penalties and Fines:

Regulatory bodies such as the Equal Employment Opportunity Commission (EEOC) in the U.S. or national labor tribunals in other countries may impose fines and penalties on companies found guilty of permitting discriminatory bullying. These fines can be substantial, particularly if the company is a repeat offender or if the behavior has affected multiple employees.

3. Reputation Damage:

In addition to financial penalties, employers face the risk of reputation damage. Lawsuits or investigations involving workplace bullying can tarnish the public image of a company, leading to negative press, decreased customer trust, and difficulties in recruiting top talent.

4. Legal Liability for Managers:

Managers and supervisors who knowingly allow workplace bullying or harassment to continue may also face personal legal liability. In some jurisdictions, individuals in management positions can be sued personally if they fail to act on harassment complaints or actively contribute to the hostile environment.

Steps Employees Can Take to Seek Legal Recourse

If internal efforts to resolve workplace bullying or harassment are unsuccessful, employees have legal avenues available to protect their rights. Here's how employees can pursue legal recourse:

1. File an Internal Complaint:

The first step is to follow the company's procedures for filing an internal complaint. This typically involves submitting a formal report to Human Resources or a designated compliance officer. Keep detailed documentation of all incidents of bullying, including dates, times, individuals involved, and any correspondence or evidence (e.g., emails or texts).

2. Seek External Legal Assistance:

If the company fails to take adequate action, employees can seek the guidance of a labor or employment attorney. A lawyer can help the victim assess the severity of the case, determine whether legal grounds for a lawsuit exist, and advise on the best course of action.

3. File a Complaint with Government Agencies:

Depending on the country or region, employees can file a formal complaint with a government agency that oversees labor and discrimination laws. For example:

   a. **In the United States,** employees can file a complaint with the Equal Employment Opportunity Commission (EEOC) for workplace harassment or discrimination.
   b. **In the United Kingdom,** employees can bring their case to an employment tribunal.

c. **In the European Union,** complaints can be filed with national equality bodies or labor tribunals that enforce anti-discrimination laws.

These agencies will investigate the claims and may mediate between the employee and the employer or bring the case to court.

4. Collective Action:

If multiple employees are facing similar harassment or bullying from the same perpetrator or within the same toxic environment, they may consider filing a class action lawsuit. This allows a group of employees to combine their claims, presenting a stronger case against the employer and ensuring that multiple victims are represented.

5. Whistleblower Protections:

Many jurisdictions provide whistleblower protections for employees who report bullying, harassment, or other forms of misconduct. These laws protect employees from retaliation, such as being fired or demoted, for speaking out. For example, the Whistleblower Protection Act in the U.S. and similar laws in the EU ensure that employees who report illegal behavior are safeguarded from adverse consequences.

Key Legal Protections for Employees.

Employees should be aware of the legal protections available to them, including:

1. **Anti-discrimination laws:** Ensure that individuals are not harassed or discriminated against based on protected characteristics such as race, religion, gender, or age.

2. **Health and safety regulations:** Require employers to provide a safe workplace, free from harassment or intimidation that could cause emotional or physical harm.
3. **Retaliation protections:** Prevent employers from retaliating against employees who report workplace bullying, harassment, or discrimination. Employees who face retaliation can file additional legal claims.

By knowing their rights and the legal framework surrounding workplace bullying, employees can take informed steps to protect themselves and seek justice if internal resolution efforts fail.

©Workplace bullying and harassment can escalate into serious legal issues if they cross into discrimination or lead to significant harm. Both employees and employers should be aware of the legal consequences that accompany unchecked toxic behavior. While victims have legal recourse through lawsuits, regulatory bodies, and anti-discrimination laws, the best approach is for companies to proactively address and prevent such behaviors. By fostering an environment of respect, openness, and accountability, organizations can avoid legal consequences and create a safer, more supportive workplace for all employees.

3. What Should the Victim Do?:

a. **Document Everything:** Keep a detailed record of all incidents of harassment or intimidation. Note dates, times, people involved, and the specific nature of the behavior. If emails or messages are part of the harassment, save them as evidence.
b. **Report the Behavior:** If direct confrontation with the bully is not an option, or if the bullying persists, escalate the issue to HR or a manager. Follow the company's official procedures for filing a complaint.

c. **Seek Support:** Don't face it alone. Speak to trusted colleagues, friends, or family for emotional support, and consider seeking professional counseling if the bullying takes a toll on your mental health.
   d. **Know Your Rights:** Familiarize yourself with company policies regarding harassment and workplace bullying. In many regions, there are also legal protections in place for victims of workplace harassment.

4. How Should Managers Handle Workplace Bullying?:

   a. **Take Every Complaint Seriously:** Managers should never dismiss claims of bullying or intimidation as "office politics." Every complaint should be investigated thoroughly, and the victim should feel supported and protected during the process.
   b. **Intervene Early:** Addressing toxic behavior early on can prevent it from escalating. Managers must be proactive in resolving conflicts and setting clear expectations for respectful behavior in the workplace.
   c. **Enforce Anti-Bullying Policies:** Companies should have clear policies regarding bullying and harassment, with defined consequences for violations. Managers must ensure these policies are not only in place but actively enforced.
   d. **Foster an Inclusive Environment:** Encouraging open communication, celebrating diversity, and providing ongoing training on inclusivity and respect can help create a culture where bullying is less likely to thrive.

Conclusion:

Workplace bullying and intimidation, particularly when it involves instigating hatred against a colleague, is a serious issue with far-reaching consequences. It affects the victim's emotional and mental health, as well as the overall functioning of the organization. Both employees and managers have a role in addressing and preventing bullying. By fostering a culture of respect, openness, and accountability, toxic behaviors can be identified and eliminated before they take root.

CHAPTER 5

Mental Health in a Toxic Environment

The Toll of Toxicity on Mental and Emotional Health.

Toxic work environments can have a profound impact on an individual's mental and emotional well-being. The constant exposure to stress, negativity, and unhealthy dynamics takes a cumulative toll, often manifesting in physical and psychological symptoms. For many employees, the relentless pressure of working in such environments can lead to burnout, anxiety, depression, and a host of other mental health challenges.

The emotional toll of a toxic workplace often includes:

a. **Chronic stress:** The constant need to navigate toxic relationships, micromanagement, or unreasonable demands can lead to chronic stress, affecting both mental and physical health.

b. **Anxiety and fear:** Employees in toxic environments may experience a persistent fear of being reprimanded, excluded, or mistreated, which leads to heightened anxiety and worry, even outside of work hours.

c. **Low self-esteem:** Toxic environments erode employees' confidence, especially when they are subjected to criticism, belittlement, or unfair comparisons to others.
d. **Depression:** Over time, the negative atmosphere can lead to feelings of hopelessness, helplessness, and disengagement. Many employees in toxic work environments feel trapped, unable to see a way out, and may even question their professional worth.
e. **Physical symptoms:** Mental health issues often manifest physically, with symptoms such as headaches, insomnia, digestive issues, or a weakened immune system. Long-term exposure to toxicity in the workplace can contribute to severe health problems like heart disease or hypertension.

In this section, the focus is on how workplace toxicity creates an unhealthy mental load and the signs that your mental health might be deteriorating due to the environment. Understanding this toll is crucial to taking the next steps toward protecting and prioritizing your mental well-being.

How to Protect Your Mental Well-Being:

Protecting your mental health in a toxic work environment requires intentional strategies to buffer yourself from the negative effects while maintaining your professionalism. Although it may be impossible to immediately change the environment, there are proactive steps you can take to safeguard your well-being.

1. Set Boundaries: Learn to say no when necessary. Establish clear professional boundaries with toxic colleagues or managers, particularly in terms of workload and communication. It's important to protect your time and energy, especially if demands are unreasonable.

2. Take Breaks: When work becomes overwhelming, step away—whether it's a short walk, deep breathing exercises, or simply taking a few moments to clear your head. Regular breaks help reset your stress levels and allow for mental recovery.

3. Practice Self-Care Outside of Work: Make sure that you are investing time in activities that promote relaxation, joy, and well-being. Exercise, hobbies, mindfulness practices, and spending time with loved ones are essential for recharging emotionally and mentally. These practices build your emotional resilience to withstand workplace toxicity.

4. Cultivate a Support Network: Build relationships with colleagues, friends, or family members who can offer support, encouragement, and perspective. Sometimes simply talking about what you are experiencing can help reduce the emotional burden.

5. Maintain Perspective: Toxic environments can cloud your judgment, making you feel as though things will never improve. It's important to maintain perspective and remind yourself that this job does not define your worth. Reflect on your skills, successes, and personal strengths to keep a positive view of yourself and your future.

This section is designed to provide you with actionable tips and exercises for protecting your mental health, including journaling, mindfulness techniques, and ways to create a healthy work-life balance despite a negative environment.

The Role of Therapy and Counseling.

When the impact of workplace toxicity becomes too overwhelming, seeking professional help can be a game-changer. Therapy and counseling offer a safe space to process your experiences, develop coping mechanisms, and manage the emotional fallout of toxic work environments.

Therapists and counselors can provide support in several key areas:

1. **Identifying patterns:** Sometimes, we are too close to a situation to recognize how it's affecting us. A therapist can help you see patterns in your behavior or thoughts that may be contributing to your stress or anxiety.

2. **Coping strategies:** Professional counselors offer tools to help you cope with toxic environments, such as cognitive-behavioral techniques to manage negative thoughts, stress reduction exercises, or communication strategies for handling difficult colleagues.
3. **Building confidence:** Toxic environments often strip employees of their self-worth. Therapy can help rebuild your confidence and give you a clearer sense of your personal value, separate from the negative work environment.
4. **Managing boundaries:** If setting boundaries has been challenging, therapy can offer guidance on how to assert yourself in difficult situations and maintain healthier work-life boundaries.

Additionally, many employers offer Employee Assistance Programs (EAPs) that provide confidential counseling services. These resources can be invaluable for employees struggling with mental health issues related to their work environment.

This section will explore how to find the right therapist or counselor, the benefits of professional mental health support, and ways to access these services—either through workplace programs or external resources.

Building Resilience and Coping Mechanisms.

One of the most empowering responses to a toxic work environment is building personal resilience. Resilience doesn't mean accepting or tolerating toxicity, but it does mean developing the inner strength to cope with difficult situations without being overwhelmed by them. Building resilience allows you to stay mentally strong and resourceful, even when external circumstances are challenging.

Here are some strategies for building resilience:

1. Develop Emotional Intelligence: Understanding and managing your emotions is key to thriving in difficult situations. Emotional intelligence helps you remain calm under pressure, respond to conflicts constructively, and handle difficult people without taking things personally.

2. Reframe Negative Situations: Cognitive reframing is a powerful tool that involves shifting how you perceive a negative situation. Instead of feeling defeated by a toxic colleague or manager, try viewing their behavior as a reflection of their issues, not your worth. By reframing challenges as opportunities for growth, you can maintain a sense of control and empowerment.

3. Focus on What You Can Control: Toxic environments often leave us feeling powerless. Instead of focusing on what you can't change (e.g., management or organizational culture), focus on what you can control, such as your work ethic, attitude, and self-care. This shift in focus can reduce feelings of helplessness.

4. Practice Gratitude: Even in the most negative environments, there are moments of positivity. Practicing gratitude helps rewire your brain to focus on the good in your life. This doesn't mean ignoring toxic behaviors, but it allows you to keep perspective and maintain a positive outlook.

5. Learn Stress-Management Techniques: Techniques such as deep breathing, meditation, progressive muscle relaxation, or visualization can help lower your stress response in high-pressure situations. These coping mechanisms help you navigate the daily stresses of a toxic environment without feeling overwhelmed.

6. Plan for the Future: If your work environment is unsustainable, start planning for an exit strategy. Having a clear plan for your next steps—whether it's looking for a new job or developing skills to move into a different role—can help you feel more empowered and less trapped.

This section offers practical advice on how to build resilience, from developing mindfulness practices to focusing on personal growth and creating strategies for future success. It is designed to encourage you to take control of your mental and emotional health, even in challenging circumstances.

Summary of the Chapter:

In this chapter, we explore the mental health toll of working in toxic environments, from the emotional impacts to physical symptoms. Readers will learn strategies to protect their mental well-being, including setting boundaries, cultivating self-care habits, and maintaining perspective. We also discuss the role of therapy and counseling in providing professional support, and offer tools for building resilience and effective coping mechanisms that can help readers navigate toxicity with strength and clarity. Ultimately, the chapter emphasizes the importance of taking proactive steps to protect mental health while working toward long-term solutions.

CHAPTER 6

Breaking Free
How to Escape or Manage a Toxic Environment

---••—•—••---

Knowing When to Leave vs. When to Stay:

One of the most challenging decisions to make when facing a toxic work environment is determining whether to stay and try to improve the situation or leave for the sake of your well-being. Staying in a toxic environment too long can lead to severe mental, emotional, and physical harm, but leaving a job isn't always immediately feasible. Balancing financial responsibilities, career aspirations, and personal well-being requires careful consideration.

Here are some key factors to consider when deciding whether to stay or leave:

a. **Assess the severity of the toxicity:** If the work environment is causing significant harm to your mental or physical health, it may be time to prioritize your well-being. Are you constantly anxious, depressed, or overwhelmed due to work? Is the toxicity affecting your personal life and relationships? In these cases, leaving may be the best option.

b. **Consider your financial and career situation:** Can you afford to leave immediately, or would it be wiser to develop a transition plan while still employed? Evaluate whether your current role is essential for your long-term career goals or if staying could harm your professional development.

c. **Evaluate potential for change:** Are there opportunities to improve the environment through direct action, such as speaking to management or HR, or by altering your own strategies for dealing with the toxicity? If you believe the situation could improve with intervention, it might be worth staying and attempting to resolve the issues.

d. **Identify red flags that signal it's time to leave:** Consistent feelings of burnout, a lack of respect or support from management, systemic discrimination or harassment, and persistent emotional or physical health issues related to work are strong indicators that it's time to exit the environment.

This section is designed to guide you through the difficult decision-making process of whether to stay or leave, offering tools to evaluate their current circumstances and long-term goals.

Practical Strategies for Managing Toxicity if You Can't Leave.

If leaving is not an immediate option, it's essential to develop strategies for managing the toxicity while protecting your well-being. There are ways to navigate a toxic environment without letting it consume you, even when an exit isn't feasible in the short term.

1. Create a Mental and Emotional Buffer: Distance yourself emotionally from the toxic elements of the environment. Visualize a mental barrier between you and the negativity around you. This buffer can help you focus on your tasks without internalizing the toxicity or letting it affect your emotional state.

2. Limit Exposure to Toxic Individuals: If certain colleagues or managers are the source of the toxicity, try to limit your interactions with them whenever possible. Focus on professional interactions, keep conversations brief and focused on work, and avoid unnecessary contact.

3. Stay Grounded in Your Values: Toxic environments can cause you to question your self-worth or professional values. Regularly remind yourself of your skills, achievements, and values. By focusing on your own integrity and what you stand for, you can reduce the influence of the toxicity on your sense of self.

4. Document Incidents: Keep a record of any toxic behaviors, such as bullying, harassment, or unreasonable demands. Documenting these incidents with specific dates and details can help if you need to escalate the issue to HR or seek legal action in the future.

5. Focus on What You Can Control: In toxic environments, it's easy to feel powerless. Instead, focus on the aspects of your work you can control—your own performance, time management, and personal boundaries. By directing your energy toward these elements, you can maintain a sense of agency.

6. Develop an Exit Strategy: If staying is a necessity for the time being, start planning your eventual exit. Update your resume, network with professionals in your field, and explore job opportunities discreetly. Having a clear plan for leaving can provide mental relief, knowing that you have a way out in the future.

7. Self-Care is Non-Negotiable: Prioritize self-care both inside and outside of work. This could mean setting boundaries around work hours, engaging in stress-relief activities like exercise or mindfulness, or finding hobbies and personal interests that bring you joy and balance outside of the workplace.

This section is designed to provide you with practical tools to endure toxic environments without sacrificing your health or values, empowering them to stay strong and focused even in challenging circumstances.

How to Approach Human Resources and Management for Support.

When a work environment becomes toxic, it's critical to know how and when to escalate issues to Human Resources (HR) or management. Taking the step to report toxic behavior can be intimidating, but it's often necessary to create accountability and initiate change. Before approaching HR or management, it's essential to prepare effectively.

1. Document Everything: Before initiating a formal complaint, make sure you have a clear and detailed record of the toxic behavior. Include dates, times, specific incidents, and any communications (emails, messages) that illustrate the problem. Having concrete evidence strengthens your case and helps HR or management address the issue effectively.

2. Know Company Policies: Familiarize yourself with your organization's policies regarding workplace behavior, discrimination, harassment, and other relevant issues. Understanding these policies ensures that you frame your complaint within the appropriate context and know your rights as an employee.

3. Frame Your Complaint Professionally: When approaching HR or management, focus on the impact of the toxic behavior on the work environment rather than making personal accusations. Use objective language and explain how the toxic behavior is affecting your productivity, team morale, and overall workplace harmony.

4. Be Clear About What You Want: Before approaching HR or management, think about what resolution you're seeking. Are you asking for mediation, a formal investigation, or specific changes in behavior? Having a clear goal will help the conversation stay focused on finding solutions.

5. Stay Calm and Professional: While it's understandable to be emotionally affected by workplace toxicity, try to remain composed during your conversations with HR or management. This professionalism will strengthen your position and help you communicate more effectively.

6. Follow Up: After reporting the issue, keep track of how HR or management is addressing your concerns. If there's no action or progress after a reasonable period, don't hesitate to follow up and request updates on the situation.

7. Know When to Seek External Help: If HR or management fails to address your concerns, or if you feel that reporting the issue internally has put you at risk for retaliation, consider seeking legal advice. Labor laws, including EU and COA laws, protect employees from toxic work environments, harassment, and retaliation. If internal processes don't provide a resolution, external legal assistance might be necessary.

This section is designed to guide you through the formal process of approaching HR or management, providing practical tips on how to present their case professionally, avoid common pitfalls, and follow up to ensure that appropriate actions are taken.

Why You Should Report Workplace Bullying and Discrimination to HR:

A Balanced Perspective

It's true that many employees are reluctant to report workplace bullying or discrimination to HR because of a widely held belief that HR departments primarily exist to protect the company's interests. While it's understandable that employees may feel cautious, it's crucial to recognize that reporting to HR is not only a formal and necessary step in addressing toxic workplace behavior but also often the most effective means of initiating change. Here's why:

1. HR's Dual Role: Supporting Both Employees and the Organization

Human Resources departments are indeed responsible for protecting the company's interests, but part of those interests includes maintaining a safe, respectful, and legally compliant workplace. Companies are legally obligated to prevent and address workplace bullying, discrimination, and harassment. If HR fails to address such issues, the organization risks legal liability, reputational damage, and high turnover rates, all of which are harmful to the business.

HR's job is not just to protect the company but to also enforce policies that support a healthy and productive work environment. In fact, the company's long-term success is directly tied to creating a positive workplace culture, and HR plays a key role in achieving this. Therefore, addressing reports of bullying and discrimination is in HR's best interest as much as it is in the employee's.

2. HR Is Legally Obligated to Address Workplace Harassment and Discrimination

Under employment and labor laws in many jurisdictions, HR departments are legally mandated to investigate and resolve reports of workplace bullying, harassment, and discrimination. Failure to do so can result in significant legal consequences for the company, including lawsuits, financial penalties, and reputational damage. Employees who file complaints with HR create a formal record that the company must address, or they risk violating labor laws and employment regulations.

This legal obligation means that HR cannot simply ignore complaints to protect the company. When an issue is formally reported, it activates a legal responsibility** for HR to conduct an investigation and take appropriate corrective action.

3. Reporting Creates a Formal Record and Accountability

When you report workplace bullying or discrimination to HR, you create a formal paper trail that holds the company accountable. Without formal documentation, it's much easier for bullying and discrimination to be brushed aside or ignored. Filing a report is not only a way to raise awareness of the issue but also a step that forces the company to take action.

   a. **Documentation ensures accountability**: Once you report, HR must document the complaint and follow certain protocols to address the issue. This means that your report becomes part of an official record, making it much harder for HR or management to ignore the issue.
   b. **Protection for employees:** Formal complaints can also protect employees in case of retaliation. If an employee faces retaliation for reporting, they have the documented complaint as evidence, which can be crucial in any legal proceedings.

4. Reporting to HR Is a Necessary Step Before Legal Action

While it's true that HR may not always solve the issue to your satisfaction, reporting workplace bullying and discrimination to HR is a critical step in the legal process. Most labor laws require employees to exhaust internal complaint procedures, such as reporting to HR, before pursuing external legal action.

If you don't report the issue to HR first, you may undermine your ability to pursue legal recourse later. By reporting the issue formally, you show that you attempted to resolve the problem within the company, which strengthens your case if legal action becomes necessary.

5. HR Departments Are Often Changing for the Better

In recent years, there has been a growing recognition that employee well-being is central to organizational success. Many HR departments are redefining their role to be more supportive of employees, not just the company. This shift is partly driven by increasing attention to workplace culture, mental health, and employee retention. Reporting workplace issues is part of driving this change. When employees speak up, it forces HR departments and organizations to confront issues they may not have fully recognized.

Many companies are also investing in training HR professionals to handle workplace bullying, discrimination, and harassment more effectively, ensuring that investigations are conducted fairly and that corrective measures are implemented appropriately.

6. You're Not Just Helping Yourself – You're Helping Others

By reporting bullying and discrimination, you're not just standing up for yourself—you're potentially helping others who may be experiencing the same mistreatment. Workplace bullying and discrimination rarely affect just one person. Toxic behaviors often go unchecked because employees fear retaliation or believe that nothing will change. When you report, you break the silence and may encourage others to come forward, prompting HR to take the issue seriously and address it on a broader level.

Changing workplace culture: One report may not seem like it will shift the workplace dynamic, but collective reports and accountability can lead to widespread cultural change. You can help create a safer, more respectful workplace not just for yourself but for your colleagues as well.

Debunking the Myth That HR Only Protects the Company.

It's easy to think of HR as solely protecting the company's interests, but this viewpoint is oversimplified. HR's role is to maintain the balance between employee well-being and the organization's legal and operational needs. When HR departments function effectively, they foster a productive, safe, and legally compliant work environment, which benefits both employees and the company. Reporting workplace bullying or discrimination is not only about getting justice for yourself—it also ensures that HR fulfills its role in promoting a healthy, respectful workplace culture.

Conclusion: Reporting is Empowerment

By reporting workplace bullying and discrimination to HR, you are:

1. Documenting the issue and creating accountability.
2. Ensuring the company is legally obligated to address your concerns.
3. Protecting yourself and potentially laying the groundwork for future legal recourse.
4. Helping others who may also be experiencing similar issues.
5. Driving positive change in the company's culture by making HR aware of toxic behaviors that need addressing.

"While it's true that HR's role can sometimes feel aligned with protecting the company, it's also designed to protect the company by ensuring it adheres to laws and regulations that safeguard employees. By reporting, you are engaging in a process that can protect you and others and potentially lead to meaningful change in your workplace."

Summary of the Chapter:

In this chapter, you will learn to make the difficult decision of whether to stay or leave a toxic work environment, offering guidance on how to evaluate the severity of the situation and your own well-being. For those who cannot leave immediately, practical strategies are provided for managing toxicity, such as limiting exposure to negative influences, protecting mental and emotional health, and planning for a future exit. Finally, the chapter offers a detailed guide on approaching HR and management to address toxic behaviors, including how to document incidents, communicate professionally, and seek resolution while safeguarding their rights.

CHAPTER 7

Legal Rights and Workplace Protections (EU and COA Law)

───··─●─··───

Understanding Your Legal Rights in the EU and Under COA Law:

Employees working in toxic environments often feel trapped, believing they have no recourse for dealing with unfair treatment, harassment, or unsafe work conditions. However, under European Union (EU) law and COA (Council of Arbitration) law, there are legal protections in place to ensure that employees have the right to a safe and non-toxic work environment. These laws are designed to protect workers from harassment, discrimination, and unfair treatment, as well as provide remedies if their rights are violated.

1. EU Labor Laws:

The EU has enacted various laws aimed at protecting employees' rights. Some key pieces of legislation include:

Detoxification: Toxic Work Atmosphere

1. **The EU Charter of Fundamental Rights:** This legal framework protects workers from workplace discrimination and guarantees rights such as the right to fair working conditions, equality, and dignity at work.
2. **The Framework Directive on Safety and Health at Work (Directive 89/391/EEC):** This directive requires employers to ensure the safety and health of their employees by identifying and addressing risks in the workplace, which includes managing toxic work environments.
3. **The Equal Treatment Directive (2006/54/EC):** This directive prevents discrimination based on gender, and extends protection to cover harassment and sexual harassment in the workplace.
4. **The Whistleblower Protection Directive (2019/1937):** This legislation protects employees who report misconduct or illegal activities in their organization, safeguarding them from retaliation.

2. COA Law:

The Council of Arbitration (COA) sets out its own set of regulations that apply to disputes in specific industries or regions, often focusing on arbitration and mediation for conflict resolution. If your organization or industry falls under COA jurisdiction, you may have additional protections or avenues for resolving workplace disputes, such as arbitration panels or mediation services to address toxic work environments.

3. Key Protections Under These Laws:

1. **Protection from Discrimination:** You have the right to a workplace free from discrimination based on race, gender, age, disability, religion, or sexual orientation.
2. **Protection from Harassment:** Whether it's bullying, verbal abuse, or sexual harassment, EU and COA laws provide you with the legal grounds to report such behavior and seek recourse.

3. **Right to a Safe Work Environment:** Employers are obligated to ensure that your workplace is physically and emotionally safe. This includes creating policies to prevent toxicity, addressing employee complaints, and mitigating risks that may lead to psychological harm.
4. **Protection from Retaliation:** If you report toxic behaviors such as harassment or discrimination, you are protected from retaliation by your employer under EU and COA law. Employers are prohibited from punishing employees who come forward with legitimate concerns about workplace toxicity.

This section will walk you through the key legal protections available under EU and COA law, providing an accessible guide to the rights and safeguards employees have when faced with a toxic work environment.

©How to Document and Report Toxic Behavior Legally.

If you are experiencing toxic behavior in the workplace, it is essential to document your experiences thoroughly and accurately. Proper documentation is crucial if you decide to report the issue to Human Resources, management, or seek legal action. Clear and organized records can substantiate your claims and provide evidence in support of your case.

©Here's how to document toxic behavior legally:

1. Keep Detailed Records:

a. **Record incidents immediately:** As soon as an incident occurs, write down as much detail as possible. Include the date, time, location, people involved, and a description of what happened.

b. **Be specific:** Avoid vague language. Instead of writing, "My boss was rude to me," provide details such as, "On July 3rd at 10:30 a.m., my boss said, 'You're incompetent and can't handle this job,' in front of the entire team."
c. **Include supporting documents**: Save emails, text messages, or any written communication that illustrates toxic behavior. For example, if a manager sends a demeaning email or if there's evidence of unfair treatment through work schedules or project assignments, include those as part of your documentation.

2. Maintain a Record of Your Work Performance:

Toxic managers may attempt to discredit your work as a form of retaliation. Keeping a detailed record of your job performance, including positive feedback, projects completed, and any performance reviews, will help counter any false claims about your work.

3. Log Witness Accounts:

If any colleagues witnessed the toxic behavior, make a note of who was present. If possible, ask them to provide written statements about what they observed. Witnesses can be key in supporting your case, especially if the behavior was public.

4. Follow Company Procedures for Reporting:

Before reporting the behavior externally, follow your company's internal procedures. Most organizations have guidelines for reporting harassment, discrimination, or other forms of misconduct. By adhering to these protocols, you can show that you tried to resolve the issue within the company before escalating further.

5. Submit Reports in Writing:

When you report toxic behavior to HR or management, make sure to do it in writing. This creates a paper trail that can be referenced later if the issue escalates or if there is any dispute about what was reported. Use clear, factual language, and avoid making emotional or accusatory statements. Simply state the facts and the impact the behavior has had on you or the team.

By following these steps, you can ensure that your documentation is professional, thorough, and legally sound. This section will also include templates for documenting toxic incidents, ensuring that readers have a clear guide to gathering and organizing their evidence.

When and How to Involve Legal Counsel.

In some cases, internal reporting and management intervention may not be enough to address workplace toxicity. If the situation escalates, if your rights are violated, or if your job is threatened due to retaliation, it may be necessary to involve legal counsel.

1. When to Seek Legal Help:

a. **Severe Harassment or Discrimination:** If you are facing serious harassment or discrimination based on your gender, race, sexual orientation, or any other protected characteristic, it's essential to involve legal counsel sooner rather than later.

b. **Retaliation for Reporting:** If you've reported toxic behavior and are facing retaliation—such as demotion, unfair dismissal, or negative performance reviews—it's time to seek legal advice.

c. **HR or Management is Unresponsive:** If you've followed your company's reporting procedures and HR or management has failed to act, or if they are protecting the toxic individuals, seeking external legal help may be necessary.

d. **Physical or Mental Health Impact:** If the toxic environment is causing serious harm to your physical or mental health and you need time off or other accommodations, a lawyer can help ensure that your rights under EU and COA labor laws are upheld.

2. How to Involve Legal Counsel:

   a. **Consult with an Employment Lawyer:** Employment lawyers specialize in labor law and can provide you with advice on how to proceed based on your situation. They can help you understand your legal rights, guide you through the documentation process, and represent you in legal disputes.
   b. **Present Your Documentation:** When you meet with legal counsel, bring all your documentation, including records of toxic behavior, written complaints to HR or management, and any responses you received. This will help your lawyer assess the strength of your case.
   c. **Consider Mediation or Arbitration:** In some cases, lawyers may recommend mediation or arbitration as a way to resolve disputes without going to court. Mediation allows both parties to work with a neutral third party to come to an agreement, while arbitration involves a more formal process in which an arbitrator makes a binding decision.
   d. **Pursue Legal Action:** If mediation fails or is not appropriate, legal counsel can help you file a formal complaint or lawsuit against your employer. This might include claims for wrongful termination, discrimination, harassment, or violation of workplace safety laws.

This section is designed to provide you with guidance on how to find the right legal representation, what to expect during the legal process, and how to protect your rights throughout. I emphasized the importance of taking legal action only when necessary, but encourage you to know that you have recourse if your workplace becomes untenable.

Mercedes E.O. Monden

Summary of the Chapter:

In this chapter, you will learn about your legal rights under EU and COA law, ensuring you understand the protections available against workplace discrimination, harassment, and unsafe conditions. You will be guided through the steps of documenting and reporting toxic behavior in a legally sound way, making their case more credible and effective. Finally, the chapter offers a comprehensive guide on when and how to involve legal counsel, including seeking advice from employment lawyers and considering mediation or legal action when necessary. This chapter empowers you to stand up for your rights in the face of workplace toxicity, with clear steps for protecting yourself legally.

CHAPTER 8

Recognizing and Confronting Discrimination

───── ·•─●─•· ─────

Forms of Workplace Discrimination (Gender, Race, Age, etc.)

Discrimination in the workplace comes in various forms and can deeply affect both individuals and the overall work environment. Discrimination occurs when employees are treated unfairly or unequally based on characteristics that are legally protected under anti-discrimination laws. These characteristics include, but are not limited to, gender, race, age, disability, sexual orientation, religion, and ethnicity. Understanding the different forms of discrimination is key to recognizing when it is happening and knowing how to confront it effectively.

Here are some common forms of workplace discrimination:

a. **Gender Discrimination:** Unequal treatment based on gender, often seen in wage disparities, exclusion from promotions, or biased performance evaluations. This can also include sexual harassment or inappropriate comments based on gender stereotypes.

b. **Racial and Ethnic Discrimination:** Discrimination based on an individual's race or ethnic background, including being passed over for promotions, unequal pay, racial slurs, or exclusion from professional development opportunities. This also extends to stereotypes or assumptions about work capabilities based on race.

c. **Age Discrimination:** Often targeted toward older employees, age discrimination includes being denied career opportunities due to perceptions of being "too old" for certain roles, or conversely, younger workers being passed over for jobs because they are seen as inexperienced.

d. **Disability Discrimination:** Treating an individual unfairly because of a physical or mental disability, or failing to provide reasonable accommodations that would enable them to perform their job duties effectively.

e. **Religious Discrimination:** Discrimination based on an individual's religious beliefs or practices, including being penalized for requesting time off for religious holidays, being forced to conform to certain practices, or being harassed for religious expressions.

f. **Sexual Orientation and Gender Identity Discrimination:** This form of discrimination targets individuals based on their sexual orientation or gender identity. Examples include homophobic or transphobic remarks, unequal treatment in hiring or promotions, and a hostile work environment toward LGBTQ+ employees.

In this section, you will learn about the different ways discrimination manifests in the workplace and the importance of understanding these categories to better recognize when you or others are being unfairly treated.

How to Spot Systemic Discrimination.

Systemic discrimination refers to deeply ingrained biases and unequal treatment that are built into the policies, practices, and culture of an organization. Unlike individual acts of discrimination, systemic discrimination is often harder to detect because it operates at a structural level. It may not involve explicit harassment or slurs, but rather, subtle patterns of exclusion and bias that affect certain groups disproportionately over time.

Here are some signs of systemic discrimination:

a. **Unequal opportunities for advancement:** If certain groups (e.g., women, minorities, older employees) are consistently overlooked for promotions or leadership positions, despite their qualifications, it could be a sign of systemic bias.

b. **Pay disparities:** A persistent pay gap between employees of different genders, races, or other protected categories is often a clear indicator of systemic discrimination. If people with similar qualifications are being paid differently, there may be underlying discriminatory practices at work.

c. **Lack of diversity in leadership:** If the leadership of an organization is overwhelmingly homogeneous (e.g., predominantly white men), it may reflect systemic barriers that prevent others from advancing into leadership roles. This lack of diversity can perpetuate discriminatory practices within the company culture.

d. **Unequal disciplinary actions:** If employees from certain groups are disproportionately reprimanded, demoted, or dismissed, while others receive more lenient treatment for similar behavior, this could point to systemic discrimination.

e. **Stereotyping in job assignments:** Employees from certain backgrounds may be pigeonholed into specific roles based on stereotypes, such as women being assigned more administrative tasks or minorities being given less visible positions.

f. **Unconscious bias in performance reviews:** When performance evaluations consistently favor one group over another—whether in terms of praise, promotion, or professional development—this may signal systemic bias in how work performance is assessed.

In this section, we will explore case studies and examples that highlight how systemic discrimination manifests in different organizations. Recognizing these patterns is the first step in addressing larger structural issues within an organization, and this chapter is designed to equip you with the knowledge to spot systemic bias early on.

Strategies for Addressing Discriminatory Behavior Legally and Internally.

Confronting discrimination in the workplace can be daunting, but there are concrete steps you can take to address the issue both legally and within the company. Whether you are experiencing discrimination directly or witnessing it happen to others, understanding your options for addressing the behavior is key to creating change.

1. Addressing Discrimination Internally:

1. **Speak Up Early:** If you feel safe to do so, address discriminatory behavior directly with the individual involved. Sometimes, discriminatory comments or actions stem from ignorance rather than malice, and a respectful conversation can correct the behavior before it escalates.
2. **Report to Management or HR:** If direct confrontation isn't an option or the behavior continues, report the issue to your supervisor, manager, or HR department. Most companies have anti-discrimination policies in place, and HR is tasked with investigating these complaints.

Detoxification: Toxic Work Atmosphere

3. **Follow Company Procedures:** Make sure to follow your organization's reporting procedures when addressing discrimination. This might involve filing a formal complaint or attending mediation sessions. Keep written records of all interactions, including responses from management or HR.
4. **Gather Allies:** If others in your workplace are experiencing similar discrimination, consider coming together to report the issue collectively. A group complaint is often harder to ignore and can prompt swifter action from management.

2. Legal Strategies for Addressing Discrimination:

1. **Document Incidents:** Like toxic behavior, it is essential to document all instances of discrimination. Include dates, times, who was involved, and any witnesses or supporting materials such as emails or performance reviews that reflect biased treatment.
2. **File a Complaint with the Appropriate Authorities:** If internal procedures do not resolve the issue, you can escalate by filing a formal complaint with external authorities. In the EU, this might include your country's labor tribunal or human rights commission. Each country has its own agencies for handling workplace discrimination, such as the Equality and Human Rights Commission (EHRC) in the UK or the Federal Anti-Discrimination Agency in Germany.
3. **Know Your Legal Rights:** Under EU law, you are protected from discrimination based on gender, race, age, religion, disability, and other protected characteristics. Additionally, you are protected from retaliation for reporting discrimination. If your employer attempts to retaliate by demoting, firing, or penalizing you in any way, they are violating the law, and you have the right to seek legal recourse.
4. **Seek Legal Counsel:** Employment lawyers specialize in discrimination cases and can advise you on your options, including potential settlements, arbitration, or litigation. They can also help

you navigate the complexities of EU and national anti-discrimination laws to ensure your rights are protected.
5. **Consider Mediation:** In some cases, legal counsel may suggest mediation as a way to resolve the issue without going to court. Mediation allows both parties to come together with a neutral third party to negotiate a resolution, which could include policy changes, disciplinary action, or compensation.

3. Escalation Through Public or Legal Channels:

1. **Use Whistleblower Protections:** If the discrimination you're facing is part of a larger, systemic issue, such as fraud, legal violations, or widespread discriminatory practices, consider whistleblower protections. The EU Whistleblower Directive (2019/1937) offers protection from retaliation for employees who report wrongdoing within their organization.
2. **Take Legal Action:** If all internal and mediation options fail, you may need to pursue legal action through the courts. This can result in remedies such as compensation for lost wages, punitive damages, or changes in company policies and practices to prevent future discrimination.

In this section, you will learn practical steps for addressing discrimination both internally and through legal channels. Templates for filing formal complaints and guidelines for how to approach these conversations professionally and effectively will be provided.

Summary of the Chapter:

In this chapter, you have learn to recognize the different forms of workplace discrimination, including gender, racial, age, and disability discrimination, among others. You have also learn how to spot systemic discrimination, which operates on a structural level, often through unconscious bias and unequal opportunities. Finally, the chapter is provided to clear, actionable strategies for addressing discriminatory behavior—both internally through HR and management, and externally through legal action or whistleblower protections. By understanding the full scope of their rights and options, you are empowered to confront discrimination and foster a more inclusive work environment.

CHAPTER 9

Combating Racism in the Workplace

––––––– ··•—●—•·· –––––––

The Persistent Issue of Racial Discrimination.

Racial discrimination remains one of the most pervasive forms of inequality in the workplace, affecting employees of color in both overt and subtle ways. Despite the implementation of anti-discrimination laws, racial bias continues to manifest in various aspects of professional life, from recruitment to promotion, and even in everyday interactions. Racial discrimination creates barriers for minority employees, not only in career advancement but also in achieving a sense of belonging and respect in their workplace.

Racial discrimination in the workplace can take many forms, including:

   a. **Hiring Bias:** Employers may consciously or unconsciously favor certain racial or ethnic groups in hiring, which can result in fewer opportunities for qualified minority candidates. This is often reflected in a lack of diversity in leadership roles or key departments.

b. **Unequal Pay and Opportunities**: Employees of color often face disparities in pay, despite having similar qualifications and experience as their white counterparts. They may also be passed over for promotions or high-profile projects, reinforcing racial inequalities within the organization.
c. **Hostile Work Environment:** Some employees face overt racism in the form of racial slurs, derogatory comments, or exclusion from team activities. This creates a hostile work environment that can lead to emotional distress and disengagement.
d. **Microaggressions:** Unlike overt racism, microaggressions are subtle, often unconscious remarks or actions that communicate negative stereotypes or biases. Examples include repeatedly mispronouncing someone's name, making assumptions based on race, or implying that a person's success is a result of affirmative action rather than their own merit.

Understanding the forms of racial discrimination is critical in order to recognize its presence and take action. This section will discuss the various ways racism can manifest in the workplace and the systemic structures that allow it to persist.

Real-Life Cases of Racism at Work

One of the most effective ways to illustrate the ongoing issue of racism in the workplace is through real-life cases. These stories highlight how racial discrimination unfolds in different industries and positions, affecting employees' mental well-being, career progression, and overall quality of life. The following case studies are representative examples of common challenges faced by employees of color in the workplace:

Mercedes E.O. Monden

Case 1: Hiring Discrimination in the Tech Industry

A qualified Black woman with an extensive background in software development applied for multiple positions at a prominent tech company. Despite her qualifications, she was passed over for roles she was highly suited for, while less experienced white male candidates were hired. After several rejections, she found out through a former colleague that internal discussions around her "cultural fit" were used to justify the decisions, despite her technical expertise. The company's lack of diversity in its workforce reflected systemic hiring bias that disproportionately affected minority candidates.

Case 2: Microaggressions in Corporate Finance

An Asian-American employee at a financial firm repeatedly faced microaggressions from colleagues and managers, including comments like, "You speak such good English for someone from your background" and assumptions that he would prefer roles involving data analysis rather than client interaction. Although these remarks were framed as compliments, they reinforced harmful stereotypes and affected his confidence in pursuing leadership roles. Over time, the cumulative effect of these microaggressions led him to disengage from his work.

Case 3: Wage Disparities in Healthcare

A Black nurse discovered that she was being paid significantly less than her white colleagues, despite having more years of experience and comparable qualifications. After raising the issue with HR, she was met with dismissive responses and told that her performance evaluations were "average," though she had consistently received positive feedback from patients and colleagues. This unequal treatment not only affected her financially but also left her feeling devalued and demotivated.

These real-life examples reveal how racism operates in both overt and subtle ways within organizations. By learning from these cases, you will gain insight into how racial discrimination impacts different aspects of professional life, and the importance of recognizing and addressing these injustices.

Tools and Resources for Fighting Racism in Your Organization

Addressing and eliminating racism in the workplace requires both individual and collective effort. Organizations must commit to creating an inclusive and equitable work environment, and employees must have access to the tools and resources necessary to confront and combat racial discrimination.

1. Diversity, Equity, and Inclusion (DEI) Programs:

- DEI programs are designed to foster a culture of inclusion by raising awareness about racial bias, promoting diverse hiring practices, and creating opportunities for underrepresented groups. Effective DEI initiatives should include:

    a. Training and workshops on recognizing unconscious bias and racism.
    b. Mentorship programs that provide guidance and support for employees of color.
    c. Clear diversity goals that are monitored and reported regularly.
    d. Affirmative action policies to ensure equal opportunities for all employees, particularly in leadership and decision-making roles.

2. Employee Resource Groups (ERGs):

- ERGs are voluntary, employee-led groups that focus on creating a sense of community for minority employees within an organization. They provide a platform for employees of color to voice concerns, network, and support each other, as well as promote awareness of racial issues within the broader workforce. ERGs often work closely with HR and leadership to influence policy changes that promote diversity and inclusion.

3. Anti-Racism Training:

- Anti-racism training goes beyond diversity awareness to actively address and dismantle racist structures within the workplace. These training sessions educate employees on how racism manifests in organizational practices and policies, as well as equip them with the tools to challenge racist behaviors and decisions. Anti-racism training is a critical step toward creating a more equitable workplace, where all employees feel safe and respected.

4. Anonymous Reporting Channels:

- Having an anonymous reporting system in place allows employees to report incidents of racism or discrimination without fear of retaliation. These systems can be used to flag inappropriate behavior, document recurring issues, and prompt investigations into discriminatory practices. Ensuring that such systems are accessible and taken seriously by leadership is key to promoting accountability within the organization.

5. Regular Audits of Hiring and Promotion Practices:

- Organizations should conduct regular audits of their hiring, promotion, and compensation practices to identify any patterns of racial bias. This can include reviewing diversity statistics at different levels of the organization, analyzing wage gaps across racial groups, and assessing whether certain groups are being disproportionately affected by layoffs or disciplinary actions. Transparency in these audits, combined with corrective actions, can go a long way in addressing systemic racism.

6. Inclusive Leadership:

- For meaningful change to occur, leadership must be committed to combating racism at all levels of the organization. Leaders should be trained on how to promote diversity and inclusion, actively seek input from employees of color, and hold themselves accountable for fostering an equitable workplace. This includes ensuring that people of color are represented in decision-making roles and that their perspectives are valued in shaping company policies.

7. External Resources and Partnerships:

- Many organizations partner with external advocacy groups and consulting firms that specialize in anti-racism and diversity initiatives. These partnerships can help provide an objective perspective on how to improve internal policies and practices, as well as offer expertise on effective anti-racism strategies. Additionally, partnering with organizations like the Racial Equality Council or Black Lives & All Lives Matter can demonstrate a company's commitment to broader social justice causes.

In this section, you will be provided with practical tools and resources that can be used to combat racism in their workplace. Whether advocating for stronger DEI programs, implementing anonymous reporting systems, or pushing for inclusive leadership, these strategies can help employees and organizations take active steps toward eradicating racial discrimination.

Mercedes E.O. Monden

Summary of the Chapter:

In this chapter, we address the persistent issue of racial discrimination in the workplace, discussing the ways it manifests through hiring bias, pay disparities, microaggressions, and hostile work environments. Real-life case studies illustrate the lived experiences of employees facing racism, highlighting the emotional, financial, and professional tolls it takes. Finally, the chapter provides you with tools and resources for combating racism within their organizations, from DEI programs and employee resource groups to anti-racism training and anonymous reporting channels. By actively engaging with these strategies, both employees and leaders can contribute to creating a more equitable and inclusive work environment.

CHAPTER 10

Pros and Cons of Exposing Toxicity

The Potential Consequences of Whistleblowing or Addressing Toxic Behavior

Exposing workplace toxicity or becoming a whistleblower is a significant decision that can have wide-ranging consequences. While bringing toxic behavior to light can lead to positive changes, such as creating a healthier work environment and holding individuals accountable, there are also risks involved. Before taking action, it's crucial to understand the potential outcomes—both positive and negative—so you can make an informed decision.

Potential Pros of Exposing Toxicity:

a. **Creating Change:** Bringing attention to toxic behavior can lead to improved policies, better leadership practices, and a healthier work environment. This can benefit not only you but also your colleagues, especially those who may not feel empowered to speak up.

b. **Holding Individuals Accountable:** When toxic managers or colleagues go unchecked, they often continue harmful behaviors, impacting more employees. By exposing the problem, you create a pathway for management or HR to address the situation and hold individuals accountable for their actions.

c. **Strengthening the Organization:** Toxicity negatively impacts productivity, morale, and employee retention. By exposing the issue, you can help the organization recognize and address problems that may be undermining its overall success. In some cases, companies are unaware of how deep the toxicity runs, and whistleblowing can provide a necessary wake-up call.

d. **Personal Empowerment:** Taking a stand against toxicity can empower you personally, knowing that you are standing up for what is right. Many individuals find a sense of fulfillment and pride in challenging unjust behaviors, regardless of the outcome.

Potential Cons of Exposing Toxicity:

a. **Retaliation:** Despite legal protections, whistleblowers often face retaliation from their employers or colleagues. This can manifest as demotions, exclusion from key projects, negative performance reviews, or even termination. Some organizations may attempt to silence or discredit the whistleblower, making it difficult to continue working in the same environment.

b. **Strained Relationships:** Exposing toxic behavior can strain relationships with colleagues, particularly if others are complicit or fearful of being associated with the issue. You may face social isolation, reduced collaboration, or hostility from those who feel threatened by the exposure.

c. **Career Impact** Depending on how the situation unfolds, whistleblowing can impact your career trajectory. In some cases, the individual may feel forced to leave the organization or face difficulties finding new employment, especially if their reputation is damaged as a result of speaking out.

d. **Emotional and Psychological Stress:** The process of exposing toxicity, especially if it involves legal action or prolonged conflict, can be emotionally draining. Dealing with retaliation, workplace politics, and the uncertainty of the outcome can contribute to stress, anxiety, or burnout.

This section will provide real-life examples of the pros and cons faced by whistleblowers and those who have addressed toxic behavior in their organizations. Understanding the full spectrum of potential consequences will help you make a more informed decision before taking action.

How to Weigh the Risks and Rewards of Speaking Up

Deciding whether to speak up about toxicity in the workplace is a deeply personal choice, and it's important to weigh the risks and rewards carefully. While the decision to expose toxic behavior may ultimately depend on your specific circumstances, there are some key factors to consider when making your choice.

1. **Assess the Severity of the Toxicity:** Is the behavior or environment causing harm to your mental or physical health, or that of others? How pervasive is the toxicity, and how long has it been going on? If the toxicity is severe or affecting multiple people, the rewards of exposing it may outweigh the risks.

2. **Consider Your Position:** Do you have the influence or support to address the issue effectively? Sometimes, those in leadership positions or with stronger networks may be better equipped to expose toxicity with less risk of retaliation. Conversely, if you're in a vulnerable position (e.g., new to the company, in a non-permanent role), the risks may be higher.

3. **Review Company Culture:** Evaluate how your organization handles conflict, whistleblowing, or issues of toxicity. Does the company have a track record of supporting employees who speak up, or are whistleblowers often retaliated against or ignored? A company with a transparent, supportive HR process will likely handle reports of toxicity better than one with a more closed-off or punitive culture.

4. **Identify Legal Protections:** Research your legal protections under employment laws, such as whistleblower protection or anti-retaliation statutes. In the EU, for example, the Whistleblower Protection Directive ensures that employees who report illegal or unethical activities are shielded from retaliation. Knowing your rights can help you determine whether you are in a strong position to report toxicity.

5. **Evaluate the Impact on Your Career:** Consider how speaking up might affect your professional future. Will exposing toxicity improve your work environment and open up new opportunities? Or could it lead to strained relationships, demotions, or even job loss? While it's essential to act with integrity, it's also important to think about your long-term career goals.

6. **Plan for Worst-Case Scenarios:** Before speaking up, prepare for worst-case outcomes. What will you do if you face retaliation, such as a demotion or job loss? Having an exit strategy or a contingency plan, such as exploring new job opportunities or building a strong network of professional contacts, can provide you with peace of mind.

By carefully weighing the risks and rewards, you can make an informed decision about whether exposing the toxicity is worth the potential fallout. This section will offer practical exercises and decision-making frameworks to help guide you through this process.

Building Alliances and Support Systems in the Workplace.

When preparing to address toxic behavior in the workplace, building alliances and support systems is critical. You don't have to go through this process alone. By building a network of colleagues who share your concerns or support your values, you create a buffer of support that can help you withstand the challenges of exposing toxicity.

Here are key strategies for building alliances and support systems:

1. Find Like-Minded Colleagues: Chances are, if you are experiencing toxic behavior, others are too. Reach out to colleagues you trust and see if they share similar concerns. Sometimes, gathering a group of individuals with shared experiences can give your report more weight and create a united front.

2. Join or Start Employee Resource Groups (ERGs): Many organizations have ERGs that focus on diversity, inclusion, and employee well-being. Joining these groups can provide you with support, resources, and advice from others who may have dealt with similar issues. If your organization lacks such groups, consider starting one with the help of HR or management.

3. Engage with HR or Management Early: If possible, engage HR or management in the early stages of addressing toxicity. They may be able to offer guidance on the best way to handle the situation, including mediation or other conflict resolution tools. Be sure to document these conversations and follow formal procedures to ensure accountability.

4. Seek Mentors or Advisors: Having mentors or advisors, either within your organization or outside of it, can be invaluable when navigating workplace toxicity. These individuals can provide objective advice, help you strategize, and support you as you move forward. Look for individuals with experience in handling workplace challenges, and who have the influence or knowledge to guide you through this process.

5. Leverage External Networks: Building alliances outside of your immediate workplace can also be helpful. Networking with professionals in your industry or joining professional organizations allows you to gain perspective, advice, and possibly even alternative opportunities if things don't improve in your current role.

6. Use Legal Counsel as a Support System: In cases where you believe you are at significant risk of retaliation, engaging legal counsel early can help protect your rights. A lawyer can advise you on how to approach your employer, document incidents correctly, and take necessary legal action if needed. Knowing that you have legal backing can provide additional confidence as you expose toxic behavior.

7. Self-Care and Emotional Support: Addressing workplace toxicity can be emotionally taxing, so it's important to take care of your mental health throughout the process. Engage in self-care practices that help you manage stress and anxiety, and lean on your personal support systems—friends, family, or a therapist—to help you cope with the emotional toll of speaking up.

This section will provide practical strategies for building alliances, creating networks of support, and leveraging mentorship to strengthen your position when confronting toxicity in the workplace.

Detoxification: Toxic Work Atmosphere

Summary of the Chapter:

In this chapter, you will learn about the pros and cons of exposing workplace toxicity. While bringing toxic behavior to light can lead to positive changes, such as holding individuals accountable and improving the work environment, it can also carry risks like retaliation and career damage. The chapter is designed to guide you through the process of weighing the risks and rewards of speaking up, helping you make informed decisions based on their unique situation. Finally, it will offer strategies for building alliances and support systems in the workplace, emphasizing the importance of having a network of colleagues, mentors, and external resources to navigate the challenges of exposing toxicity.

CHAPTER 11

Rebuilding After the Toxicity

―――――― ·•— •—•· ――――――

What to Do After Leaving a Toxic Workplace

Leaving a toxic workplace can be both a relief and a challenge. While you've removed yourself from an unhealthy environment, the effects of the toxicity can linger emotionally, mentally, and even physically. The first step after leaving is to recognize the importance of allowing yourself time to recover and reset.

Here are some practical steps to take after leaving a toxic workplace:

1. Take Time to Reflect: It's crucial to take a moment to reflect on your experience. This is not about dwelling on the negativity but understanding what happened, what you learned from the situation, and how it affected you. Reflecting on your experience allows you to process it and identify what needs to be healed. Ask yourself:

  a. What patterns of toxicity were present?
  b. How did I cope with those challenges?
  c. What could I do differently in future situations?

2. Disconnect and Decompress: Toxic work environments are draining, often leaving you emotionally and physically exhausted. After leaving, take time to decompress—whether that means taking a break, going on a trip, or simply allowing yourself a period of rest and recovery. Disconnecting from the toxic environment helps you regain perspective and energy for the future.

3. Reclaim Your Identity: Toxic workplaces often strip employees of their confidence and sense of professional identity. Start the process of rebuilding by reconnecting with your strengths, values, and passions. Reflect on what drives you professionally and how you can reconnect with your goals in a way that aligns with your values.

4. Update Your Resume and Skills: After leaving, take the opportunity to update your resume, highlighting your achievements and accomplishments in your previous role, despite the challenges of the environment. If you feel that the toxicity held you back from growing, consider taking courses or pursuing certifications that can enhance your skills and broaden your opportunities in your next role.

5. Network and Rebuild Relationships: Rebuilding after a toxic work environment can sometimes feel isolating, especially if you had strained relationships with former colleagues. Start reconnecting with your professional network, reaching out to former coworkers or mentors who were not part of the toxic environment. Attend industry events or join professional organizations to re-engage with the broader community in your field.

This section will help guide you through the practical and emotional steps to take after leaving a toxic workplace, ensuring that you focus on healing and regaining your professional footing.

How to Heal and Move Forward Mentally and Professionally

Healing after a toxic work experience is essential for both your mental well-being and future career success. Toxic environments can leave deep emotional scars, affecting your confidence, trust in others, and overall outlook on work. Moving forward requires an intentional approach to mental healing and professional reinvention.

1. Acknowledge the Emotional Impact: Toxic workplaces can take a significant emotional toll. Acknowledge the feelings of frustration, anger, or hurt you may have experienced. Suppressing these emotions can lead to burnout or affect your ability to trust future colleagues. Give yourself permission to feel, process, and heal from these experiences.

2. Seek Professional Support: Therapy or counseling can be invaluable in helping you work through the emotional fallout of a toxic workplace. A mental health professional can help you process the experience, rebuild self-confidence, and offer coping mechanisms for dealing with future challenges.

3. Rebuild Your Confidence: Toxic work environments often erode self-esteem, making you doubt your abilities and worth. Focus on rebuilding your confidence by:

   a. Recognizing and celebrating your strengths and accomplishments.
   b. Setting small, achievable goals that help you feel in control and capable again.
   c. Engaging in activities that you enjoy and that remind you of your value outside of work.

4. Practice Self-Care: Healing is not just a mental process but a physical one as well. Engage in self-care practices that nourish your body and mind, such as exercise, meditation, journaling, or hobbies that bring you joy and relaxation. This will help reduce stress and rejuvenate your energy for the next phase of your career.

5. Redefine Your Career Path: After leaving a toxic environment, take time to redefine your career goals. What kind of work environment do you want to be in? What kind of company culture aligns with your values? This is an opportunity to seek a professional path that prioritizes both your well-being and career aspirations.

6. Practice Forgiveness: While difficult, learning to forgive those who contributed to the toxicity can be an important step in moving forward. Forgiveness doesn't mean forgetting or excusing the behavior, but rather releasing the emotional hold that it has on you, freeing you to focus on your future rather than dwelling on past negativity.

This section is designed to will provide you with actionable steps and techniques to facilitate both emotional healing and professional recovery, ensuring that you move forward from the toxicity in a healthy and empowered way.

Finding a Positive Work Environment:

Red and Green Flags

As you move forward and search for new opportunities, it's important to recognize the red and green flags that can help you evaluate the culture and health of future workplaces. Knowing what to look for will ensure that you find an environment where you can thrive both personally and professionally.

Red Flags: Warning signs of a potentially toxic work environment.

1. High Turnover Rates: If an organization has a high rate of employee turnover, it could be a sign of underlying issues such as poor management, lack of support, or a toxic culture.

2. Negative Reviews on Employer Websites: Websites like Glassdoor or Indeed often feature reviews from current and former employees. Consistently negative feedback regarding leadership, culture, or management practices is a red flag.

3. Vague or Inconsistent Communication: During the interview process, pay attention to how the company communicates. If job roles, expectations, or policies are vague or seem to change frequently, it could indicate disorganization or a lack of transparency.

4. Overworked and Unhappy Employees: During interviews or visits to the office, observe the atmosphere. If employees seem disengaged, stressed, or overworked, it might be a sign that the company prioritizes productivity over employee well-being.

5. Micromanagement: Ask questions during the interview process about leadership styles and autonomy. Companies that emphasize rigid control and frequent monitoring may have a micromanagement problem, which can contribute to toxicity.

6. Lack of Diversity: If an organization lacks diversity in leadership or across departments, this could be a sign of systemic biases or an exclusive company culture that doesn't foster inclusion or respect for different perspectives.

Green Flags: Signs of a healthy and positive work environment.

1. Employee Satisfaction: Positive reviews from current employees, low turnover rates, and a strong sense of engagement and satisfaction are indicators of a supportive and healthy workplace culture.

2. Support for Work-Life Balance: Companies that emphasize flexible work arrangements, reasonable expectations regarding working hours, and respect for personal time are often those that prioritize employee well-being.

3. Opportunities for Growth and Development: Organizations that invest in employee development through training, mentorship programs, and clear career advancement paths show a commitment to their employees' long-term success.

4. Inclusive and Diverse Workplace: A diverse leadership team and a culture that embraces inclusivity are strong indicators that the company values different perspectives and fosters a respectful environment.

5. Positive Leadership: Leaders who emphasize communication, transparency, and support for their employees are often at the core of positive work cultures. Ask about leadership styles during your interview to gauge whether the company fosters a culture of trust and empowerment.

6. Strong Support Systems: Companies that provide resources for mental health, employee assistance programs (EAPs), and open channels for feedback show that they are invested in employee well-being.

This section will help you develop the ability to spot red and green flags during their job search, ensuring you avoid repeating the experience of working in a toxic environment and instead find a place that supports their growth and well-being.

Mercedes E.O. Monden

Summary of the Chapter:

In this chapter, you will learn what to do after leaving a toxic workplace, from reflecting on your experience to reclaiming their professional identity. The chapter will offer practical steps for healing and moving forward mentally and professionally, with a focus on self-care, rebuilding confidence, and redefining career goals. Finally, you will gain insight into finding a positive work environment by identifying red and green flags during the job search, ensuring that you find a workplace that supports their growth, well-being, and long-term career success.

CHAPTER 12

Preventing Toxicity in the Future

———— ·•— •— •· ————

How Organizations Can Create Healthy, Positive Work Environments

Preventing workplace toxicity requires intentional efforts from organizations at every level. A healthy work environment is not just the absence of negativity; it's a place where employees feel valued, supported, and empowered to succeed. Companies that actively foster such environments benefit from higher employee morale, increased productivity, and lower turnover. Here are key steps organizations can take to create and sustain a positive workplace:

1. Establish Clear Values and Ethical Guidelines:

Organizations need to define and promote a strong set of core values that prioritize respect, inclusion, and collaboration. When these values are clearly communicated and integrated into everyday practices, employees are more likely to align their behavior with them. Ethical guidelines that define acceptable and unacceptable behavior should be part of the company's code of conduct and reinforced regularly.

2. Promote Transparency and Open Communication:

A transparent work culture fosters trust between employees and management. Organizations should create open communication channels where employees can voice concerns, ask questions, and provide feedback without fear of retaliation. Regular check-ins, surveys, and open-door policies help ensure that issues are addressed early before they escalate into toxicity.

3. Encourage Work-Life Balance:

A supportive work environment values employees' personal time and well-being. Offering flexible work schedules, remote work options, and respecting boundaries regarding after-hours communication promotes a healthy work-life balance. Organizations should also avoid overloading employees with unrealistic expectations, which can lead to burnout.

4. Create Inclusive and Diverse Workplaces:

Inclusivity is a key factor in preventing toxicity. Organizations that prioritize diversity and inclusion create a culture where all employees feel respected and valued regardless of their background. This includes addressing unconscious bias in hiring, promotion, and day-to-day interactions. Encouraging diversity of thought, experience, and perspective enhances creativity and collaboration.

5. Provide Employee Support Resources:

Healthy workplaces offer resources that support employee well-being, such as mental health programs, employee assistance programs (EAPs), and access to counseling or therapy. These programs show employees that their mental health is valued, and they provide necessary support for those dealing with personal or professional challenges.

6. Encourage Positive Leadership:

Toxicity often starts at the top. Organizations should promote leadership styles that emphasize empathy, communication, and support. Positive leadership focuses on mentoring employees, encouraging professional growth, and recognizing accomplishments. Training for leaders on how to manage conflict, give constructive feedback, and foster a collaborative environment is crucial in creating a positive workplace culture.

This section will outline how organizations can build and maintain positive work environments by implementing these strategies, leading to long-term cultural health and employee satisfaction.

Training for Managers and Staff on Identifying and Preventing Toxicity

Training is an essential tool in preventing toxicity in the workplace. Both managers and staff need to be equipped with the knowledge and skills to identify, address, and prevent toxic behaviors before they take root. Investing in regular training creates a proactive rather than reactive approach to workplace culture.

1. Toxicity Awareness Training for Managers:

Managers play a critical role in setting the tone for the workplace. They need to be trained to identify toxic behaviors in themselves and others. Key areas of focus include:

a. **Recognizing signs of toxic behavior:** Understanding how toxic behaviors such as micromanagement, exclusion, favoritism, and bullying manifest.
b. **Conflict resolution skills:** Managers should learn how to address conflicts constructively and prevent minor disagreements from escalating into larger issues.

c. **Effective communication**: Training managers to communicate openly, provide clear expectations, and give constructive feedback in a way that fosters growth rather than defensiveness.
   d. **Creating psychological safety:** Managers should create environments where employees feel safe to speak up, share ideas, and voice concerns without fear of negative consequences.

2. Toxicity Prevention Training for Employees:

Employees also need tools to prevent toxicity within their teams. This training helps create a culture of accountability where everyone plays a role in maintaining a positive environment. Key areas of focus include:

   a. **Recognizing toxic behaviors:** Teaching employees how to spot early signs of toxicity in themselves or their colleagues.
   b. **Practicing self-awareness:** Encouraging employees to reflect on their own behaviors and how they may contribute to the workplace atmosphere, positively or negatively.
   c. **Building communication and conflict-resolution skills:** Empowering employees to handle interpersonal conflicts with respect and professionalism, rather than allowing resentment to build.
   d. **Promoting teamwork and collaboration:** Training employees on the value of collaboration, inclusion, and diversity of thought, which can prevent divisions and cliques from forming.

3. Ongoing Training and Development:

Organizations should implement regular training sessions on workplace culture, toxicity prevention, and leadership development. This ensures that new hires are introduced to the company's cultural values, and long-term employees are reminded of the importance of maintaining a positive, supportive environment.

"By implementing training programs for managers and staff, organizations can build a culture where toxic behaviors are quickly identified and addressed, fostering a more respectful, productive workplace for everyone."

Your Role in Maintaining a Healthy Work Culture Wherever You Go

As an individual employee, you play a crucial role in maintaining and contributing to a positive work culture. While organizational policies and leadership set the framework, the day-to-day interactions and attitudes of every employee shape the overall environment. Whether you're a manager, team member, or new hire, you have the power to influence the workplace for the better.

1. Be a Role Model for Positive Behavior:

Lead by example in your interactions with others. Show respect, empathy, and professionalism in all your communications, and promote collaboration rather than competition. When others see positive behaviors consistently, they are more likely to follow suit.

2. Foster Open Communication:

Encourage honest and transparent communication within your team. If issues arise, address them directly but respectfully, focusing on solutions rather than blame. Be open to feedback and create a space where your colleagues feel comfortable sharing their thoughts and ideas.

3. Practice Self-Reflection and Accountability:

Regularly reflect on your behavior and how it affects your colleagues. Are there areas where you could improve in terms of collaboration, communication, or conflict resolution? Taking accountability for your actions and striving for personal growth is an essential part of maintaining a healthy workplace.

4. Contribute to an Inclusive Environment:

Be an advocate for inclusion and diversity. Support colleagues from different backgrounds, make space for everyone's voice to be heard, and challenge exclusionary behaviors when you see them. Creating a sense of belonging for all employees is key to a thriving work culture.

5. Encourage and Support Others:

A positive work environment thrives on mutual support. Recognize and celebrate your colleagues' accomplishments, offer help when needed, and lift others up rather than tearing them down. When employees feel supported by their peers, morale and productivity rise.

6. Be Proactive in Addressing Toxicity:

Don't ignore toxic behaviors when you see them. While it can be uncomfortable, addressing toxicity early prevents it from spreading. Speak up respectfully when you witness toxic behavior, whether it's bullying, exclusion, or unfair treatment. Encourage others to do the same and be a voice for positive change.

7. Participate in Culture-Building Initiatives:

Get involved in initiatives that promote a positive work culture, whether it's joining an employee resource group, organizing team-building activities, or offering ideas for workplace improvement. Taking an active role in culture-building strengthens your connection to the organization and promotes a sense of community.

"In this section I emphasized the importance of individual responsibility in maintaining a positive work environment. By being proactive, self-aware, and supportive, you contribute to a healthier, more enjoyable workplace for yourself and others."

Summary of the Chapter:

In this final chapter, you will learn how organizations can create and sustain positive work environments, including the importance of transparency, inclusion, work-life balance, and employee support programs. This chapter also highlights the value of training for managers and staff on identifying and preventing toxicity, offering practical ways to instill a culture of accountability and respect. Finally, you will be empowered to understand your own role in maintaining a healthy work culture, with actionable steps to lead by example, foster communication, support diversity, and be proactive in preventing toxicity wherever they go.

CONCLUSION

The Path to a Healthier Work Life

---••—•—••---

The Ongoing Journey of Detoxifying Your Work Atmosphere

Detoxifying a work environment, whether as an individual or as part of an organization, is not a one-time event but an ongoing journey. Toxicity in the workplace often grows subtly, and addressing it requires consistent effort, awareness, and a commitment to fostering a healthier culture over time. As you move forward, it's important to remember that both personal responsibility and collective action play essential roles in creating and maintaining a positive work environment.

The journey of detoxifying your work atmosphere begins with self-awareness. Recognizing how your actions, attitudes, and communication styles contribute to the work environment is key. From here, you can focus on personal growth, actively promoting positive behaviors, and encouraging collaboration and respect in your interactions. As outlined in this book, it's not just about managing others—it's about recognizing your own influence on workplace culture and committing to being a force for positive change.

On an organizational level, detoxifying the work atmosphere requires ongoing attention to policies, practices, and leadership behaviors. Companies must continually evaluate their work culture, listening to employee feedback, investing in diversity and inclusion efforts, and providing resources that support mental and emotional well-being. Addressing toxic behaviors, whether from colleagues or management, early on and systematically is crucial for long-term change.

Ultimately, maintaining a healthy work environment is a shared responsibility. It requires ongoing attention to the dynamics within the workplace, the behaviors of individuals, and the overall structure and values of the organization. When everyone works together to prioritize well-being, inclusivity, and respect, the result is a more productive, engaged, and satisfied workforce.

Final Thoughts on Creating Lasting Change.

Creating lasting change in the workplace takes dedication and persistence. The toxic behaviors that corrode work environments don't disappear overnight, and tackling them can be challenging. However, the rewards of a healthy, vibrant workplace—where everyone feels valued and motivated—are well worth the effort.

As you continue on your professional journey, keep the following principles in mind:

1. Start with Self-Awareness: Positive change begins with you. Continuously reflect on your own behaviors, recognize areas for improvement, and strive to be a leader in promoting respect, inclusivity, and transparency.

2. Empower Others: Encourage your colleagues and leaders to take ownership of creating a positive work environment. Whether through mentorship, team-building activities, or open conversations about workplace culture, empower others to take action and support a healthier atmosphere.

3. Promote Accountability: Hold yourself and those around you accountable for maintaining a respectful and supportive work environment. Toxic behaviors can take root when they go unchecked, so make sure that accountability and transparency are core values in your workplace.

4. Embrace Continuous Improvement: Building a healthy work environment isn't a one-time effort; it requires continuous improvement. Stay open to feedback, be willing to adapt, and remain committed to learning how to create a better workplace for yourself and your colleagues.

5. Seek Alignment with Values: Whether you are starting a new job or advocating for changes in your current role, ensure that your work aligns with your personal and professional values. When your values are in harmony with your work environment, you are more likely to feel fulfilled, engaged, and motivated.

6. Focus on Long-Term Success: Building a positive workplace is a long-term investment. It requires patience, perseverance, and a willingness to adapt as challenges arise. By focusing on the long-term success of both individuals and the organization, you create a foundation for lasting, meaningful change.

> *"As you move forward, remember that a healthy work environment is not just beneficial for individual well-being—it also enhances team collaboration, boosts creativity, and ultimately contributes to the success of the entire organization. By actively participating in creating a culture of positivity, respect, and inclusion, you can make a lasting impact on the workplace and your professional life."*

Final Words:

The path to a healthier work life is not always easy, but it is essential. Whether you are navigating toxicity, building a more positive environment, or seeking new opportunities, the journey of detoxification requires commitment and courage. With the tools, insights, and strategies shared in this book, you are equipped to face the challenges of workplace toxicity head-on and create a thriving, supportive professional environment wherever you go. Lasting change starts with awareness, grows with action, and is sustained by a culture that values every individual's well-being.

Take these lessons with you and remember: a healthier work life is possible, and you have the power to make it happen.

BONUS READ

Daily Affirmations for Workplace Healing

---·•—•—•·---

Strength, and Personal & Professional Identity Recovery

Workplace Healing Affirmations

1. I release any negativity from my past work experiences and open myself to new, positive opportunities.
2. I am deserving of a workplace that respects and values me for my contributions.
3. Each day, I choose to heal from the toxic experiences that once held me back.
4. I forgive myself and others for any harm caused, allowing space for peace and growth.
5. My work environment is becoming a place of harmony, respect, and collaboration.

Affirmations for Strength

1. I am strong enough to overcome any challenge that comes my way.
2. No matter what happens at work, I am grounded in my values and inner strength.
3. Each obstacle I face makes me stronger and more resilient.
4. I have the power to create positive change, no matter my circumstances.
5. My strength is not defined by my past, but by my ability to rise today.

Personal and Professional Identity Recovery Affirmations

1. I am reclaiming my professional identity, and I know my worth.
2. I am not defined by my past experiences, but by my potential for future success.
3. I deserve to pursue my career with passion, purpose, and confidence.
4. I honor the unique skills and talents I bring to the table, and I embrace my true professional identity.
5. I am becoming the best version of myself, both personally and professionally.

These affirmations are meant to be repeated daily, encouraging reflection, empowerment, and healing in your professional journey. By incorporating these into your routine, you can foster a positive mindset that will help you recover from past challenges and move forward with confidence and clarity.

Appendix

This appendix is designed to provide additional resources, references, and tools that complement the main content of *Detoxification: Toxic Work Atmosphere*. The materials here will assist you in further exploring topics covered in the book and offer guidance for practical application.

A. Self-Reflection and Personal Accountability Resources

a. **Self-Assessment Tools:** A checklist of toxic behaviors to identify whether you may be unknowingly contributing to workplace toxicity.
b. **Journaling Prompts:** Questions to help you reflect on your workplace experiences and your role in fostering a healthy work culture.
c. **Growth Mindset Exercises:** Practical exercises to help shift from defensiveness to openness and embrace personal development.

B. Mental Health and Well-Being Support

a. **Mental Health Organizations:** A list of organizations that offer counseling, support, and guidance for dealing with workplace-related stress, anxiety, and burnout, including:

Detoxification: Toxic Work Atmosphere

    b. **Mind (UK)**
    c. Mental Health America
    d. World Health Organization's Mental Health Resources
    e. Therapy and Counseling Platforms: Online platforms offering therapy services, including options for remote or workplace-specific counseling.

C. Legal Rights and Workplace Protections

    a. Key Legal Frameworks: A summary of workplace protections under:
    b. The EU Employment Directive
    c. The Civil Rights Act (US)
    d. The Equality Act (UK)
    e. **Steps to File a Formal Complaint:** A guide on how to document workplace discrimination, bullying, or harassment, and the steps to take when filing a complaint with HR or relevant legal bodies.
    f. **Resources for Legal Aid:** Organizations that provide legal assistance for workplace harassment and discrimination cases.

D. Conflict Resolution and Communication Tools

    a. **Effective Communication Techniques: A** guide to assertive yet respectful communication strategies to resolve workplace conflicts and reduce tension.
    b. **Sample Scripts for Difficult Conversations:** Templates to help you approach difficult conversations with managers, HR, or colleagues regarding toxic behavior.
    c. **De-escalation Techniques:** Methods for reducing tension during workplace confrontations or when addressing toxic situations.

E. Affirmations and Daily Practices

a. **Workplace Healing and Strength Affirmations:** A compilation of affirmations provided in the bonus section, along with additional affirmations for empowerment, resilience, and growth in both personal and professional settings.
b. **Daily Practices for Well-Being:** Suggested routines that promote mental clarity and emotional well-being, including mindfulness exercises and stress management techniques.

F. Recommended Reading

a. Books on Workplace Culture
b. The No Asshole Rule by Robert Sutton
c. Radical Candor* by Kim Scott
d. Dare to Lead* by Brené Brown
e. Mental Health and Resilience:
f. The Body Keeps the Score by Bessel van der Kolk
g. Option B by Sheryl Sandberg
h. Legal Rights in the Workplace:
i. Workplace Harassment Law by Christine Jolls

G. Contact Information for Support

a. Employee Assistance Programs (EAPs): How to access your company's EAP, which may provide free, confidential counseling and support for dealing with toxic environments.
b. Helplines:
c. National Bullying Helpline (UK)
d. EEOC (US) Helpline
e. European Agency for Safety and Health at Work Contact Information

End Notes

The following end notes provide references, additional context, and further reading related to the topics covered in ***Detoxification: Toxic Work Atmosphere.*** These notes are designed to guide readers who wish to delve deeper into specific areas and provide transparency regarding the information and resources cited throughout the book.

Chapter 1: Understanding Toxic Work Environments

- For further reading on toxic work cultures and their impact on productivity, see "The Cost of Toxic Workplaces" by Dr. Christine Porath, Harvard Business Review, 2016.

Chapter 2: The Toxic Manager

- The term "micromanagement" and its negative effects on employee morale are explored extensively in Robert Sutton's *The No Asshole Rule*, which outlines behaviors that contribute to a toxic managerial style.

Chapter 3: Recognizing Toxic Colleagues

- Research on toxic workplace behaviors and their impact on team dynamics can be found in Radical Candor by Kim Scott, which discusses how honest, direct communication can reduce workplace toxicity.

Chapter 4: Are You Contributing to Workplace Toxicity?

- For a more in-depth look at self-reflection and personal accountability in the workplace, consider Carol Dweck's Mindset: The New Psychology of Success, which explains how adopting a growth mindset can help mitigate toxic behaviors.

Chapter 5: The Impact of Workplace Toxicity on Mental Health

- The connection between workplace stress and mental health is widely covered in The Body Keeps the Score by Bessel van der Kolk, which highlights how chronic stress impacts emotional well-being.

Chapter 6: Breaking Free from Toxic Environments

- Techniques for leaving toxic work situations and transitioning into healthier workplaces are discussed in Option B* by Sheryl Sandberg, which explores resilience in the face of challenging environments.

Chapter 7: Legal Rights and Workplace Protections

a. The European Union's directives on employment rights and protections are outlined in the EU Employment Directive. For specific case law and examples, refer to the official EU employment website.

b. In the U.S., protections under Title VII of the Civil Rights Act and guidance from the Equal Employment Opportunity Commission (EEOC) provide the framework for handling workplace discrimination and harassment cases.

Chapter 8: Addressing Discrimination in the Workplace

- The Equal Employment Opportunity Commission (EEOC) provides detailed resources on handling workplace discrimination in the U.S. Visit their official website for more information: www.eeoc.gov.

Chapter 9: Combating Racism in the Workplace

- The persistent issue of racial discrimination is documented in multiple reports from the European Agency for Fundamental Rights and EEOC. See their websites for relevant data and case studies.

Chapter 10: Pros and Cons of Exposing Workplace Toxicity

- The potential risks and rewards of whistleblowing are explored in Whistleblowers: Broken Lives and Organizational Power by C. Fred Alford, which provides insight into the challenges faced by those who speak up in toxic environments.

Chapter 11: Rebuilding After a Toxic Workplace

- For more guidance on mental and emotional recovery after leaving a toxic environment, see the National Institute for Mental Health's resources on workplace stress and mental well-being.

Chapter 12: Preventing Workplace Toxicity

- Dare to Lead by Brené Brown offers excellent insights into leadership styles that help prevent toxicity and promote a healthy, open workplace culture. Brown's work on vulnerability and courageous leadership aligns with the recommendations in this chapter.

Bonus Section: Affirmations for Healing and Growth

- For additional daily affirmations and techniques for personal growth, consider reading You Are a Badass by Jen Sincero, which includes exercises for self-empowerment and resilience in challenging environments.

About the Author

Mercedes E.O. Monden is an accomplished leader, pastor, author, and advocate for personal and professional growth. With a passion for empowering individuals to fulfill their divine purpose, Mercedes has dedicated her life to guiding others through spiritual and professional challenges, helping them overcome adversity and realize their true potential.

As the founder of Breath of Holies Worldwide Outreach Ministries and Senior Pastor of Royal Crown Church, Mercedes has touched the lives of many through her faith-based initiatives, community outreach programs, and global empowerment conferences. She leads several influential movements, including Mercedes Monden Ministries, the Global Business Convention, and the Pursuit of Divine Purpose Empowerment Conferences, which inspire individuals to rise above life's challenges and find strength in their faith and purpose.

Mercedes is also the initiator of the National Prayer Chain Movement in the Netherlands, a spiritual movement dedicated to collective prayer and transformation on a national scale. Her commitment to spiritual and emotional healing is reflected in her work, as she continues to provide guidance and support to those facing challenges in their personal and professional lives.

Mercedes E.O. Monden

An advocate for healthy, positive work environments, Mercedes brings her extensive experience to the forefront in her writings. She is the author of several books, including Understanding Cultural Difference, Wealth Creation Prosperity, Fulfilling God's Purpose for Your Life Against All Odds, and Detoxification: Toxic Work Atmosphere. Her work, particularly in the area of workplace toxicity, is aimed at empowering employees to recognize, confront, and break free from harmful work environments while protecting their mental and emotional well-being.

Mercedes' leadership extends beyond ministry, as she continues to be a voice for change in addressing toxic work environments. Through her teachings, books, and conferences, she equips individuals with the tools they need to overcome toxic relationships, thrive professionally, and maintain a strong sense of purpose. With her wealth of experience and wisdom, Mercedes Monden remains a guiding force for those seeking spiritual and professional detoxification, healing, and growth.